Ron McDonald, DMin

The Spirituality of Community Life
When We Come 'Round Right

Pre-publication
REVIEWS,
COMMENTARIES,
EVALUATIONS . . .

"**B**ased on his personal experiences and his comments on them, Mc-Donald explores how he came to realize the centrality of community in his life. Don't look for a how-to-book—in truth, there is no simple how-to to creating a community—but one that takes such everyday activities as hiking, basketball, open-educational schooling, and a Quaker meeting's struggles to lift up what one can learn about community living from them. It is, profoundly, a book that suggests that one must be open and live life, as it is found, to build a sense of community. McDonald is always wise, never pushing his observations beyond their limits, yet always humble and willing to admit and learn from his own mistakes and misconceptions. Expect his insights to find a strong and loyal following."

H. Larry Ingle, PhD
Professor Emeritus of History,
University of Tennessee–Chattanooga

"**R**on McDonald has given us a gift. His book, *The Spirituality of Community Life: When We Come 'Round Right,* is a testimony to the transformative power of community life. Reflecting on his own experience of 'ordinary' communal life—sports teams, workplace, contra dance groups, professional gatherings, Quaker meetings—Ron helps the reader identify the extraordinary grace-filled workings of community itself. Using the narrative method, he weaves stories of life in community with Quaker wisdom. With his insights from pastoral theology, pastoral counseling practice, and his knowledge of group dynamics, leadership-building skills, and plain common sense, Ron has created a friendly, useful book that helps readers understand both the developmental stages of communities and skills to nurture them."

Margaret Kornfeld, DMin
Pastoral Psychotherapist
and American Baptist Minister;
Past President, American
Association of Pastoral Counselors;
Author, *Cultivating Wholeness:*
A Guide to Care and Counseling
in Faith Communities

More pre-publication
REVIEWS, COMMENTARIES, EVALUATIONS . . .

"The values of Western culture which encourage independence, self-reliance, and personal privacy have gradually eroded many of the social relationships and connections of modern society. It may be that in this culture of self-sufficiency we have lost all hope of offering any kind of response to the endemic loneliness that seems to pervade our modern world. In *The Spirituality of Community Life: When We Come 'Round Right* author Ron McDonald introduces a glimmer of hope. Perhaps not all communities and the experience of connecting to others have been lost. McDonald asks us to reconsider, and rather than preaching against the loneliness and isolation of modern values he challenges us to be awakened to our presence in communities that we may have overlooked.

The joy of this book is that rather then trying harder to convince the reader of his point the author simply tells the stories of communities from his own experience. These stories enliven the readers' imaginations, reminding us, awakening us to the communities that we may already be a part of. McDonald introduces us to his communities, from a group of strangers who become friends by 'hiking alone' and 'hiking together' on the Appalachian Trail, to a community dance, we meet the communities of this man's life and leave recognizing the creative spirit of communion already at work in ours."

Jack Holland, PhD
Assistant Professor
of Pastoral Care and Counseling,
Emmanuel School of Religion

"Ron McDonald has produced a fascinating reflection on a rich and fruitful life. His is in the genre of the confessions of Augustine: theological archeology of experiences that will resonate with many readers and who will be changed by the encounter."

Walter Wink, PhD
Professor Emeritus,
Auburn Theological Seminary,
New York

The Haworth Pastoral Press®
An Imprint of The Haworth Press, Inc.
New York • London • Oxford

NOTES FOR PROFESSIONAL LIBRARIANS AND LIBRARY USERS

This is an original book title published by The Haworth Pastoral Press, an imprint of The Haworth Press, Inc. Unless otherwise noted in specific chapters with attribution, materials in this book have not been previously published elsewhere in any format or language.

CONSERVATION AND PRESERVATION NOTES

All books published by The Haworth Press, Inc., and its imprints are printed on certified pH neutral, acid-free book grade paper. This paper meets the minimum requirements of American National Standard for Information Sciences-Permanence of Paper for Printed Material, ANSI Z39.48-1984.

DIGITAL OBJECT IDENTIFIER (DOI) LINKING

The Haworth Press is participating in reference linking for elements of our original books. (For more information on reference linking initiatives, please consult the CrossRef Web site at www.crossref.org.) When citing an element of this book such as a chapter, include the element's Digital Object Identifier (DOI) as the last item of the reference. A Digital Object Identifier is a persistent, authoritative, and unique identifier that a publisher assigns to each element of a book. Because of its persistence, DOIs will enable The Haworth Press and other publishers to link to the element referenced, and the link will not break over time. This will be a great resource in scholarly research.

The Spirituality
of Community Life
When We Come 'Round Right

Ron McDonald

THE HAWORTH PASTORAL PRESS®
Haworth Series in Chaplaincy
Andrew J. Weaver, Mth, PhD
Editor

Living Faithfully with Disappointment in the Church by J. LeBron McBride

Young Clergy: A Biographical-Developmental Study by Donald Capps

Ministering for Grief, Loss, and Death by Halbert Weidner

Prison Ministry: Hope Behind the Wall by Dennis W. Pierce

A Pastor's Guide to Interpersonal Communication: The Other Six Days by Blake J. Neff

Pastoral Care of Depression: Helping Clients Heal Their Relationship with God by Glendon Moriarty

Pastoral Care with Younger Adults in Long-Term Care by Reverend Jacqueline Sullivan

The Spirituality of Community Life: When We Come 'Round Right by Ron McDonald

Pastoral Care from the Pulpit: Meditations of Hope and Encouragement by J. LeBron McBride

The Spirituality
of Community Life
When We Come 'Round Right

Ron McDonald, DMin

The Haworth Pastoral Press®
An Imprint of The Haworth Press, Inc.
New York • London • Oxford

For more information on this book or to order, visit
http://www.haworthpress.com/store/product.asp?sku=5653

or call 1-800-HAWORTH (800-429-6784) in the United States and Canada
or (607) 722-5857 outside the United States and Canada

or contact orders@HaworthPress.com

Published by

The Haworth Pastoral Press®, an imprint of The Haworth Press, Inc., 10 Alice Street, Binghamton, NY 13904-1580.

PUBLISHER'S NOTE
The development, preparation, and publication of this work has been undertaken with great care. However, the Publisher, employees, editors, and agents of The Haworth Press are not responsible for any errors contained herein or for consequences that may ensue from use of materials or information contained in this work. The Haworth Press is committed to the dissemination of ideas and information according to the highest standards of intellectual freedom and the free exchange of ideas. Statements made and opinions expressed in this publication do not necessarily reflect the views of the Publisher, Directors, management, or staff of The Haworth Press, Inc., or an endorsement by them.

Cover design by Jennifer M. Gaska.

Library of Congress Cataloging-in-Publication Data

McDonald, Ron.
   The spirituality of community life : when we come 'round right / Ron McDonald.
      p. cm.
   Includes bibliographical references and index.
   ISBN-13: 978-0-7890-2985-0 (hard : alk. paper)
   ISBN-10: 0-7890-2985-5 (hard : alk. paper)
   ISBN-13: 978-0-7890-2986-7 (soft : alk. paper)
   ISBN-10: 0-7890-2986-3 (soft : alk. paper)
   1. Community—Religious aspects—Christianity. I. Title.

BV625.M29 2006
253—dc22
                                                 2005024735

CONTENTS

Preface   ix

Introduction   1

Chapter 1. What We're Up Against: Competition,
  Insecurity, and Growth   5

Competition Against or Competition With   5
The Creation of Insecurity   7
Growth for Growth's Sake   11

Chapter 2. The Hope for America Is on the Appalachian
  Trail   15

Chapter 3. Athletic Community: Hendrix Cross Country
  and Track, 1971-1972   23

The Weather Is Just Right   25
Don't Sweat the Small Stuff   27
Don't Stop Running Now—You're Just Entering
  Your Prime   28
Community Mentors   29

Chapter 4. Mark Class   31

Chapter 5. In His Steps   35

Chapter 6. Community and the Church Health Center   41

Chapter 7. Memphis Friends Meeting   49

Chapter 8. The Revolving Nature of Communities   67

Judaism at the Time of Jesus   68
Inclusive versus Exclusive Communities   69
The Ethical Mysticism of Jesus   71
Mystical Union and Paul   72

Orthodoxy: Institutional Christianity   78
What Difference Does This Make?   79

Chapter 9. Challenging the Powers: A Revolutionary
Pseudocommunity   **83**

Chapter 10. A Championship Basketball Team   **93**

Chapter 11. Professional Community   **99**

Hospitality   101
Discernment of Gifts   103
Opportunities for Shared Work   104
Learning to Think Differently and Be Different   105
The Call to Leadership   106

Chapter 12. Dancing to Community   **109**

Conclusion   **117**

References   **123**

Index   **125**

ABOUT THE AUTHOR

Ron McDonald, DMin, is a pastoral counselor and writer from Memphis, Tennessee. He is the author of *Building the Therapeutic Sanctuary: The Fundamentals of Psychotherapy from a Pastoral Counseling Perspective* and *Home Again: A Pilgrimage of Father and Son.*

Preface

A few years ago I was in a doctoral program with seven other men. During the course of our time together we became intimately acquainted with one another's personal struggles. We decided to have communion on the last day we would be together. In preparing for the Eucharist we asked one another to do some homework. Each man was to do something toward solving a personal difficulty and bring a report of that effort to the communion table before we ate the bread and drank the juice.

My assignment was to write a letter that I might or might not send to my mother expressing my perspective on some of the conflicts we had had. Its purpose was to help me resolve some issues.

On our last day together, we gathered and shared our reports. After a few had shared, then eaten some bread and drank some grape juice, I read my letter to them. I was surprised by my emotions and found myself crying as I read a letter that had turned quite confessional and reconciling. It was difficult to read, and on occasion, as I glanced nervously at my friends, I could see that many of them were tearful as well. Their obvious empathy was quite comforting to me.

I finished reading the letter, sighed, took a piece of bread, ate it, then took the common cup of grape juice. At first I drank only a little sip, then on a sudden impulse, I quaffed the whole thing. We all started laughing. I poured some more juice for the others, then we moved on to the next man to share. After he shared, he too quaffed the whole cup, then poured some more for the next, who did the same as well. I walked away from that experience thinking that's how life should be lived. We need to drink the whole cup—surrounded by friends.

That wasn't the first or only experience I have had with a true community, but ending our incredible experience together with *communion* planted a seed in me, for now I understood experientially that communion and community are fundamentally connected. Furthermore,

doi:10.1300/5653_a

because communion is seen primarily as a religious experience, I became deeply curious about the spiritual nature of community.

I began to understand that community happens much in the way revelation happens—spontaneously, only with eyes wide open. I started opening my eyes to experiences of community and have found communities all over the place. In fact, I have found so many communities that I felt an urge to study them, to participate more fully in them, to figure out how to help them develop, and to write about them.

This book is the fruition of the exploration that began with the communion experience during the doctoral program. It is about the dynamics of communities. Its purpose is to encourage you to more fully participate in community life, and maybe even learn how to be a leader or catalyst for community.

I have written about a number of communities for two reasons. First, they are good stories, and I'd rather tell stories than just share ideas. Second, they represent a wide variety of community experiences that I hope you can identify with. I want you to learn to recognize communities when and where they are so that you can better soak up the great sustenance they offer.

This book is a celebration of community life, but it falls short of the real thing. The real thing *is* community life. So don't just read this book. Go join a community. Take the risk. It's worth it.

Introduction

The philosopher Hegel Georg Wilhelm Friedrich believed that a *volksgeist,* or "Spirit of the People" was embodied in the culture of communities (Lavine, 1984, pp. 214-239). This Spirit was the foundation for an individual's sense of ethics. The existentialists deepened this idea when they speculated on the source of a person's consciousness. They claimed that consciousness is developed through crisis and community. Crisis thrusts one into the depths of the soul, causing one to question, reflect, seek, and develop insights that were unnecessary when one's life was stable and secure. Suffering—a form of crisis—is necessary for depth of insight as we begin our quest for wisdom and consciousness. But after having suffered once, a person learns to avoid further suffering. In the lingo of the day, we think "been there, done that." If crisis was necessary for consciousness and wisdom, then we would have to create crises to keep growing. In some ways that's what is in vogue in the business world where a contemporary motto is "If it ain't broke, break it." The reason for that is because we are a culture without true community. Lacking community, we create crisis in order to find depth.

Community is a second way to develop consciousness and wisdom. Without it we develop only out of crisis. Within community, however, we develop consciousness and depth without the pain and fatigue of crisis. Thus, if we could develop communities we would not need to create crisis. Communities not only contribute to development, they do so without the level of pain and suffering inherent in crises. They do not cause anger, conflict, or even war. A crisis causes change and forces one to develop, but often at great expense. Communities do the same peacefully. Communities are the residence of creative spirit. That's what Hegel meant with the idea of the Spirit of a People. It is a community spirit. A better way to create change, stimulate development, and deepen people than the creation of crisis exists. It is the creation of community.

doi:10.1300/5653_01

The purpose of this book is to encourage the better way: the development of community. Communities that give life to our knowledge of self and our love for life do exist, but they are not highly visible. They have been replaced and overwhelmed by a national culture that takes life: a spirit of competition, separation and insecurity, and growth that is robbing us of the recognition of true communities that give life. I believe that we all have experienced these communities, but, unnamed, they are unrecognized and therefore not fully appreciated or sought after. It is my intention to name a few such communities in the hope that it will help you identify such experiences in your own life. To name something is to possess it, to have dominion over it, and therefore to be able to nurture it and re-create it. If we were to better understand the life-giving nature of true communities we would find them and create them much more often. We would be pumping life into our nation. We would be raising the level of consciousness and wisdom. It would give us life. Communities give life.

Hegel suggests that a person's sense of ethics—the idea of what is good and his or her duty to act in accord with that ideal—comes from a dialectic between the family and civil society, which, synthesized together, becomes the developed political state, or the truth of the nation. We are first introduced to morality through our family's expectations and relationships. As we grow and develop, we interact with a larger culture with different kinds of relationships and new expectations. This civil society often stands in contrast with our family's ethics, causing us to have to choose between one ethic and another or to synthesize them into a new ethic. This synthesis of ethics is not just an individual occurrence, though. It is developed through a society's finding of a sense of unity. It is molded by the Spirit of a People until it eventually is organized into a body politic—which then governs society.

What we have in the United States at its best is rich dialogue that begins with an idea that is refined through debate and disagreement until it emerges as a better idea that unifies enough of us to allow us to govern ourselves wisely. What we have at our worst is an idea that is linked with monetary or military power that is crammed down the nation's throat in the name of party or ideological victory. The losers in these political battles then seek ways to undermine the other idea. At our worst, we do not have enough unity to govern without insecurity and force. At our best, the idea is close enough to unity that the Spirit of a People polices its implementation by social pressure, not by political force.

In other words, at our worst we are a dysfunctional, insecure mass of people who care little for those outside of our direct sphere of influence but who usually stay in line because we do not want to get in trouble. At our worse, money and power rule. At our best, we function as communities that encourage civility, understanding, compromise, and altruism. At our best government is simple and natural, because people living in true communities are naturally civil. We *need* communities. We *desperately* need communities. Learning how to create them is essential to the good life we aspire to.

In *The Silent Cry: Mysticism and Resistance,* Dorothee Soelle (2001) writes poignantly about mysticism. I used to think that mysticism was confined to those who were either somewhat crazy or who experienced major revelations. I did not qualify—except for the occasional crazy part. Soelle suggests that mystical experiences are actually common, simple, and not all that dramatic. She describes mystical experiences with nature, with sex, in common prayer, in silence, when feeling compassion—experiences that we have every day. Mystical experiences, according to Soelle, are those times when life is accented, times such as when we go outside and exclaim quietly, "My, what a beautiful day!" We might find ourselves saying about an object or music, "God, this is pretty." We might not think we are praying, but Soelle suggests that we are. She wrote *The Silent Cry* to try to redeem mysticism for us common folks. She redeemed it for me.

M. Scott Peck, mostly known for authoring *The Road Less Traveled* (Peck, 1980), also wrote an important book titled *The Different Drum: Community Making and Peace* (Peck, 1988). He writes in the introduction, "most of us have never had an experience of true community" (p. 5). Although I will use some of Peck's ideas about what makes a community and how a community is created, my purpose is, in part, to do for our understanding of community what Soelle does for mysticism. I believe that Peck is wrong. Most of us, in my opinion, *have* had an experience of true community—we just do not realize that we have. I want to redeem our common sense of community so that you find it and can name it when it happens to you. It is captured in the word *communion.* When we experience true communion, we are experiencing community.

I also want to help you understand how community happens so that you can become a facilitator of community. To that end, I'll give you a hint of what matters most in the creation of community: vision and leadership. It must have a vision that transcends the selfish concerns of the group, a vision that makes the group open to others who are different. Each of the communities I describe in this book contains such a transcendent vision. A community must also have a live wire, a person who is outgoing enough to spark the group, a person who keeps the energy high. However, this person must not be so dominant as to draw too much attention. He or she must be willing to give and take leadership, but mostly be willing to take the reins of the group life when others are vacillating. I will introduce you to a number of such leaders. Such leaders emerge from a group that simultaneously grounds the leader to the limits and reality within which the community must work.

I am going to share with you experience after experience of community. I hope you will find a great deal of wisdom in reading about them, for communities make people wiser. Most of the focus will be on the importance of having a live wire in the community. This leader draws and disseminates much of the community's electricity.

Mohandas K. Gandhi used the image of electricity to help people understand anger. He said that unchanneled anger is destructive in the same way unchanneled electricity appears in the form of lightning. Channeled and controlled, however, anger and electricity are great sources of energy. Communities, similar to electricity, have tremendous energy. Channel that energy and communities have amazing strength. They give life.

I hope that after you have read this book you will recognize communities when they spontaneously happen and have some ideas about how to channel the energy those communities offer so that their life-giving wisdom might be used well. I hope those communities, more easily recognized, help you love life, because in loving life, you will love others. You will know what love, what God, is. I sincerely hope that this book will help foster community that will change our way of life to one that is truly happy and a light to the world.

Chapter 1

What We're Up Against:
Competition, Insecurity, and Growth

This is a clash between two cultures: a national culture that is about competition, the creation of insecurity, and growth for growth's sake versus a community culture that is about simplicity and a peaceful ideal. We must look first at the national culture, for if we don't understand it, we won't be able to see clearly a better way.

COMPETITION AGAINST
OR COMPETITION WITH

In the United States competition is revered. One of the highest compliments we pay to a person is to call him or her "a real competitor." Excellence is often seen as a result of the efforts of particularly fierce competitors. It is easiest to see this in professional sports.

Michael Jordan, arguably the best basketball player in the history of the National Basketball Association, is hardly ever spoken of without the inclusion of the phrase, "He was an amazing competitor." His intensely competitive nature helped him lead men to many championships. He was also known as a very sore loser for many years. Stories are told of him angrily storming away from card games he lost and of ridiculing his less skilled teammates whom he thought might cause his team to lose. For about a year he was so upset with a couple of negative media portrayals of him that he would not talk to the media. Yet this boorish behavior was accepted because he was such an intense competitor.

At the same time, no less an authority than Phil Jackson, Jordan's championship coach during the years in Chicago, believed that

doi:10.1300/5653_02

Jordan finally became a winner when he made his team better. Jackson saw Jordan give up the idea that *he* had to win it all himself, and, at the right moment, pass to his teammates so that the whole team could win together.

Barry Bonds, the great home run hitter, often called the greatest baseball player, has never been on a championship team. Despite being revered as a great competitor, I would argue that he has undermined his own teams' successes by his inability to be a team player. Jordan finally learned to play with his teammates. Bonds hasn't, and he has not yet achieved a team championship.

The difference is that great champions finally learn the difference between competing *against* others and competing *with* others. *Competition against* is an angry, individualistic quest. *Competition with* is a team endeavor. It requires community. Competitors who compete *with* learn how to respect and care for those who help them achieve victory. Competing against others might help one achieve individualistic honors, but it rarely achieves team championships. If it does, it is usually because strong team leadership holds the team together in spite of the superstar who can't work well with teammates.

American culture is focused more on competing against than competing with. We lift up individualism to such an extent that we think of community as secondary. But, as any good coach knows, good teams almost always defeat more talented individuals who don't play well together. Community is not secondary. Community is primary, but because community is so rare in the United States we are far from achieving our true potential. We are a nation of individuals who compete against one another and then wonder why team approaches do so well.

A few years ago Volvo got a large amount of press for its team-oriented approach to building automobiles. Volvo was doing excellent in world competition, whereas American companies, far superior in resources, languished. Volvo was functioning as a team. They intentionally created manufacturing teams, and from those cooperative communities, they created excellence. The Saturn car company did well also in its earlier years for the very same reason—they created teams that created excellence.

Many examples of excellence and victories come from an American team spirit, but they are exceptions to the rule. As a rule we are a nation of individuals who compete against one another. Such competition causes early success and eventual collapse.

I first noticed this phenomenon as a college middle-distance runner. A very angry, highly motivated runner would often spring onto the competitive scene with immediate success, then, within a couple of years, burn out and quit. Inevitably such runners were those who refused to join the community of runners who competed *with* one another. These runners were those who worked together through the first two-thirds of each race, sharing the pacesetting, finding encouragement from their mutual respect, then race *against* one another only a small portion of the whole race. The angry, compete-against runner, though, would stand apart from the rest, usually set the pace, and eventually the pack would catch up and pass him. Not feeling respect (or respected); this runner would not know how to accept occasional defeat, and would quit or begin to run so tight that he would no longer run well.

It would be interesting to study Enron or WorldCom and see if this dynamic of the competitor-against is behind the early success and eventual collapse. In contrast, one of the reasons why Wal-Mart continues to do well is because its corporate culture seeks to cooperate with the local culture where its stores are located. At the same time, Wal-Mart thwarts unions because they're afraid of competition with, not understanding that competition with is a cooperative, community endeavor just as much as letting the local culture into their stores is.

THE CREATION OF INSECURITY

A second dynamic is our culture of insecurity. One of the reasons why our national leaders speak so often about our need for national security is because we are a very insecure people. It is surprising, too, because as the wealthiest and most powerful nation in the world one would think that the United States would be secure. Why are we insecure? I think we are for three reasons:

1. We all die.
2. Our leaders talk so much about our enemies as a way to mobilize their power base.
3. Our news media makes money off our fears.

Struggle with Death

The first of these—that we die—is called an existential insecurity. Because we are mortal, we are naturally insecure. This insecurity offers no exit, but one can live courageously with it, and live full lives in spite of mortality's threat. Paul Tillich (1952) called it "the courage to be." It is the courage to accept our mortality as part of life itself, part of life's design that transcends our comprehension. Simply put, death is okay. It's not something we want (unless we are in great pain), it just is, and we can live fully despite the possibility of dying before we accomplish all that we would like to achieve. In other words, insecurity is unavoidable. It is part of our existence. We can, however, live with it gracefully and courageously.

Accentuating Our Differences

Many of our leaders and much of the media do not offer a way of grace and courage but instead foster insecurity in order to consolidate power and make money. Our leaders do this by accenting differences between people rather than seeking points of commonality. They draw lines between us that make us think we are competing against one another for limited goods and services. This is done in two dominant ways. First is by making sure we know what ethnic or racial group we are part of, and second is by talking about how "our way of life" is threatened.

James Meredith, in a speech in Danbury, Connecticut, in 1984, said that the main impact of integration is that it distinguishes whites from blacks, making sure that we continue to know how we are different. Although I'm not sure he's entirely right, his assertion that we are reminded often that blacks and whites are different holds much truth. Meredith adds that he thinks that desegregation, not integration, is what civil rights is about. Desegregation is about the removal of legal barriers to equal rights and opportunities, which was the next logical and appropriate step for the liberation of blacks after being freed from slavery. Integration, he asserts, depends on the premise that we are different, and it reminds us of those differences.

When I first heard Meredith's argument it was an argument I had never heard before from anyone other than a racist, and their arguments were filled with bitterness and hatred that overwhelmed any reasonableness of their points. Meredith, however, convinced me that he was envisioning a new culture that would pay less attention to our differences.

It made so much sense to me that I stopped checking my race on forms. Of course, what difference did that make? It was hardly a drop in the bucket, but it was a way to express my opinion that integration is about different people learning to live comfortably with one another until they create a new culture. Integration, as we have witnessed it, has, as Meredith says, created two side-by-side cultures. It reinforced vestiges of segregation (such as Sunday worship services and inner-city schools) by accenting our differences, despite the removal of legal barriers.

Integration works when people stop noticing their differences, but the program of integration that Meredith criticizes—the one that reminds us of who is white and who is black—now serves more to reinforce our insecurities. It is hard to feel secure when one group is pitted against another. It is another way our culture creates the perception of conflict and the need for defeating another's agenda.

Our Way of Life

In 1990 when President George H. W. Bush began to threaten an attack on Iraq he challenged Americans to defend our way of life. I was deeply troubled by that phrase—our "way of life"—, for though I believe at root our way of life is about dialogue, freedom of speech and commerce, and civility, I also think our way of life has been popularized to be about the freedom to drive gas-guzzling cars, trucks, and SUVs and the freedom to buy, buy, buy. So, in protest, I began to ride my bicycle to work with a sign attached that said, "If my way of life is going to cause a war, I'll change my way of life." A lame protest in some ways, but it was important to me, at least.

What we mean by our way of life, however, has grown more and more important to me. Although some signs indicate that we continue to have a group of intellectuals trying to lift up the true American ideals (for example, books such as *The American Soul: Rediscovering the Wisdom of the Founders,* by Jacob Needleman [2003]), we are still a nation caught up in materialism that is creating world conflict around oil, values, and discrepancy between the rich and the poor.

Edward Gibbon (1994), author of *The History of the Decline and Fall of the Roman Empire,* wrote in his last volume, "Everything that is fortified will be attacked; and whatever is attacked may be destroyed" (p. 1075). This was one of his salient conclusions after spending more than a decade of his life immersed in the study of the Roman Empire. It is a statement that reinforces the root of American insecurity. Our focus on wealth and materialism causes us to become so possessive that we have become obsessed with security. We fortify ourselves. Of course, that fortification entices those who are on the outside looking in, coveting what we have, which we see as a threat, causing us to fortify even more. A vicious cycle is happening: acquire, secure it, entice those who are shut out, secure it better, acquire more, entice the have-nots, secure it better, acquire more, etc. Our military has much to do with this vicious cycle. Our way of life creates a high level of insecurity, so we arm ourselves to the teeth. However, no amount of military might makes us feel truly secure.

Go for the Gore

Part of the creation of this insecurity is the role of the news media. In the United States the television news media's main function is to make money, and the way it does this is to entice viewers. Our news media thinks that the best way to entice viewers is to go for what is frightening and sensational. Thus, we see and hear mainly about conflicts and sensational acts of malice. We are bombarded with episodes of violence and immorality, to the point where we have become convinced that our nation is a very violent, dangerous, and often a morally corrupt country. In addition, much of the world sees the United States that way as well—but it is not how we are. Yes, violence and immorality exists, but in 99 percent of our neighborhoods is peace, tranquility, altruism, and moral behavior.

Recently Michael Moore made a movie documentary titled *Bowling for Columbine* (2003). In it is an interesting comparison of the differences between Canada and the United States. Canadians, just as Americans, are great owners of guns, but in Canada the number of homicides by guns per capita is significantly lower than in the United States. It also appears that Canadians hardly ever lock the doors of their homes, even in the large cities. Why? One reason is because Canadian newscasts do not "go for the violence" as American newscasts do. Canadians are not bombarded by frightening images as Americans are. Thus, they appear to be less insecure than Americans.

The United States is a deeply insecure nation. To try to create security we have pumped money and energy into policing ourselves and protecting ourselves with military might. It is not working! A better way would be to confront the sensationalized media that lifts up images that foster insecurity instead of presenting a more balanced and realistic view of the United States.

GROWTH FOR GROWTH'S SAKE

Paul Wachtel published a book in 1989 titled *The Poverty of Affluence: A Psychological Portrait of the American Way of Life.* Wachtel argues that by focusing so much attention on the value of growth, we have created our own dissatisfaction with what we have and where we are. He writes,

> We have established a pattern in which we continually create discontent, and we attribute the restless yearning to the spontaneous expression of human nature. . . . Growth, progress, the idea of "more" is so much a part of our consciousness that it takes very little to persuade us that any particular item is something we want or need. (pp. 18-19)

In other words, by never being satisfied with what we have, we are never content. Our focus on growth, progress, and the idea of "more" makes us fundamentally unhappy, always seeking more than what we need. This may be great for the national economy, but we pay a terrible psychological price. Though our economy grows, we do not find contentment, but discontentment.

I used to believe greatly in growth, but Wachtel changed my mind. It now makes sense to me that growth for growth's sake creates a fundamental dissatisfaction with what I have. An Italian folktale selected and retold by Italo Calvino (1956) and myself that illustrates this point.*

---

*The story is adapted from *Italian Folktales,* selected and retold by Italo Calvino (New York: Pantheon Books, 1956, pp. 117-119). The ending is my own creation.

THE HAPPY MAN'S SHIRT

A king had an only son that he thought the world of. But this prince was always unhappy. He would spend days on end at his window staring into space.

"What on earth do you lack?" asked the king. "What's wrong with you?"

"I, myself, don't even know, Father."

The king tried in every way imaginable to cheer him up, but theaters, balls, concerts, and singing were all useless, as were the many gifts he showered his son with.

Day by day the rosy hue drained from the prince's face, until, as often happens with those who are unhappy, the prince became ill. The sicker he grew, the unhappier he became, which made him sicker and unhappier. It became clear to the king that his son would die of unhappiness.

The king issued a decree, and from every corner of the earth came the most learned philosophers, doctors, and professors. The king showed them the prince and asked for their advice. The wise men withdrew to think, then returned to the king. "Majesty, we have given the matter close thought. Here's what you must do. Find a truly happy person, a person who is happy through and through, and exchange your son's shirt for his. This will make your son happy and he will live."

That same day the king sent ambassadors to all parts of the world in search of a happy person.

A priest was taken to the king. "Are you happy?" asked the king.

"Yes, indeed, Majesty."

"Fine. How would you like to be my bishop?"

"Oh, Majesty, if only it were so!"

"Away with you! Get out of my sight! I'm seeking a person who is happy just as he is, not one who is trying to better his lot."

Thus the search resumed, and before long a banker was brought before the king who claimed that he was truly happy.

"Good," said the king, "Then how would you like to be treasurer of my kingdom and live in the splendor of my palace?"

The man's eyes bugged out and he nodded, "I would, indeed!"

"Away with you! You, too, are not truly happy, for you are not happy with what you have."

Many others were brought before the king, but upon being offered wealth or power, one of which each person desired, the king would send them away.

Meanwhile, the prince grew sicker and sicker.

Exasperated, the king himself went searching for a truly happy person. Alas, he was no more successful than his ambassadors.

Late one day as the king was sadly walking back to the palace after another unsuccessful day of searching for a truly happy person, he heard someone whistling in the woods beside the road. Saying to himself, "Let me try one more person today," he left the road for the woods and soon found a young man dressed in a jacket and pants tending his garden beside a simple shack.

"Good afternoon, Majesty," said the youth with a smile.

"Bless you!" replied the king. Then he asked, "Young man, are you happy?"

"Certainly."

"Are you *truly* happy?"

"I suppose I am."

"Then would you like to tend the palace garden and live in the palace with me?"

"Thank you, Majesty, I will do so if you ask, but I prefer to stay here and tend this garden. I greatly enjoy watching it get better each year."

"Well, I appreciate that, but would you like to oversee all the lands of my kingdom?"

"I will at your bidding, Majesty, but I much prefer my simple life. I think perhaps someone else would serve you better than I."

"Then you *are* a truly happy person, for you are content with what you have! Listen, young man. Will you do me a favor?"

"With all my heart, Majesty, if I can?"

The king, unable to contain his joy any longer, ran to the young man and began unbuttoning his jacket. All of a sudden the king's arms fell to his side, and he slumped to the ground, for the young man had no shirt on.

"Where is your shirt?"

"I gave it away. I met a man who had no shirt, and since I have this jacket, I gave him my shirt."

"But I needed that shirt," replied the king in despair. "My son needed that shirt."

The king sat upon the ground in silence for a few moments, then he looked up at the youth with a look of revelation. He stood up, took the youth's hand and said, "Thank you, young man. I know what to do now."

With a spring in his step and a smile on his face, the king walked back to the palace, into his son's room, and said, "Son, I have something for you."

His son rolled weakly over to face his father, who was unbuttoning his own shirt. The king took the shirt off his son's back, replaced it with his own, which made his son smile for the first time in years.

From that point on his son was happy, got well, and lived a long, happy life.

Analysis of the Story

The king was searching for happiness from someone else, something outside of himself. Despite all his power and wealth, this was one thing he believed he did not possess. He had to find someone who possessed something he didn't have. But when he met a youth who possessed such happiness, one who was willing to even give the shirt off his own back to a stranger, the king finally understood what was called for. He understood that happiness was from within, that what his son most needed was a truly happy and vulnerable father, not possessions and entertainment. He discovered the source of his own happiness—that he himself could be truly happy were he to give of himself.

If only we could all understand as much. Perhaps our quest for material things, security, and growth would diminish and be replaced by true happiness. We are a culture caught up in a cycle of unhappiness. We try to create happiness by buying new possessions, new inventions, new luxuries. We try to overcome our insecurity by policing those whom we are afraid of and by threatening our "enemies" with military might. We focus so much on growth that we cannot be satisfied with what we have. We cannot find happiness in such a way.

Yes, we do need change. Change, in fact, will happen, for change is part of the universe. Will it be change that gives us wisdom and happiness, or will it be change that just gives us more of the same nagging unhappiness? If we keep trying to fine tune our "way of life" by more material objects, by a stronger police and military, and by getting bigger, we will not save ourselves. We will die of unhappiness. We need change that helps us be satisfied with what we have—both materially and inwardly.

How do we find such change? Well, if the pending crisis does not get us there, maybe community can. As for me, I have experienced enough crises in my life that I prefer community.

Chapter 2

The Hope for America
Is on the Appalachian Trail

In my experience, communities are normally found when people are seeking a better way or are in service to others. In both cases community members share a common motif—they are on a pilgrimage. They are seeking to find something new and better. Often they do not know what they will find, but they expect to be transformed by it.

Presented first is a story of what I consider to be a pure pilgrimage, a literal journey to find something inward, to be changed.

My oldest son, Jonah, set off on the Appalachian Trail from Mount Katahdin, Maine, in the summer of 2002, heading for Georgia. He left home alone, carrying a backpack that would top sixty five pounds once he filled it with water and food for the notorious 281-mile trek through the Maine woods. Taking public transportation and a backpacker's guidebook, he was nervous about going on the trail alone, but he met some other pilgrims even before setting off on the trail.

The Appalachian Trail traverses over 2,000 miles of rugged terrain from Maine to Georgia. Every year, it is estimated that three to four million pilgrims set out on the trail to hike, many in search of insight or serenity. Hundreds hike the whole trail and are called "2,000-milers." Those who are seeking to hike the whole trail at once call themselves "thru-hikers" (Appalachian Trail Conservancy, 2005). It has become a pilgrimage for many, most of whom are not really sure of what they are seeking, but the lure of such a feat of endurance in some of the United States' wildest lands touches a deep yearning to be transformed by discipline and challenge.

Jonah wrote us an e-mail the day before setting off for the trail.

doi:10.1300/5653_03

June 21, 2002
Hello friends,

I am writing on Friday morning, June 21st, 2002, to tell you that I am leaving Memphis for the next 5 months to begin hiking the Appalachian Trail at noon today.

Let me tell you some about my philosophy of hiking the trail: first, my main goal over the next several months is to hike. Finishing the trail and such linear goals are only secondary for me. Instead, I'm looking at this trek as more of a pilgrimage for myself—a trip in which the process is more important than the end. I do not know what I will find in this journey, but I am open to whatever may come (even if it means stopping my hike early). I am searching, but for what I'm not exactly sure. Wisdom will come from the trail, from within myself, and from the people I meet along the way. My trip is not about conquering a 2000+ mile trail, but rather it is about allowing this trail to nurture my mind and spirit.

About logistics . . . I will be safe. I promise you. I have a medicine kit and common sense. As my friend Jason tells me, just because you have a full pack doesn't mean you leave your brain at home.

I'm quite nervous about my trek. It'll turn out fine I'm sure, but that doesn't soothe my nerves much. . . . I'll just have to get out there, start hiking, and enjoy myself. I'm going to miss being in easy contact with my friends and family, but if you will hold me in the light (as we Quakers do), your love will help a huge amount. I'll be thinking of you when I'm on the trail and I hope to see you or hear from you over the next 5 months.

Until Monson, Maine . . .

Love, Jonah

Jonah began the trail alone, but in all of his six months on it, he probably spent three nights alone. He found early on that hikers like to go their own paces, so most days were spent hiking alone, but spots existed during the day and every night where hikers preferred to congregate. Most nights were spent at designated camping spots consisting of a three-sided shelter or lean-to. Some hikers slept inside the shelters, others in tents nearby. These shelters were wonderful places for sharing stories and food and for relaxing after ten to twenty miles of hiking. They were community gathering places.

I hiked with Jonah and some of his friends—four men and two women—for three days and four nights in September, and what I saw was much more than physically fit men and women. I saw people who might someday change the way we live. They were doing something that few in this country take the time to do: contemplate with body and mind a new way of being. They were learning not only how to truly live a simple life—which is, behaviorally at least, one of the greatest needs we have in this country—but also how to live in community.

Beginning with only a backpack of sustenance—food, clothing, and shelter—on their backs, they had all discovered how much less they needed than what they began with. All of them had gotten rid of pounds of irrelevant, unnecessary items, lightening their loads considerably. Jonah now carried only forty pounds. He was now built like a world-class distance runner—all long muscles, no fat. (Thru-hikers joke that the description for any man on the trail is "skinny with a beard.") When I arrived in Palmerton, Pennsylvania, I found skinny people with long hair, ragged clothes, and a great spirit about them. It was obvious to me from the start of my three days and four nights with Jonah and his new friends that they had something special. It began with introductions: everyone had a nickname: Rockhopper, Ice Cream, Ten Percent, Autumn Leaves, Bashful, and Stitches. Each name was based upon a story from that hiker's life. It made them easier to remember. The naming appeared to me to accept the hiker into the community, and it offered the newly named hiker a new identity—one that was wrapped up in mutual watchfulness, sharing, and common understanding of the difficulties (and sometimes dangers) of trail life.

They talked in ways that few people do. They were thinking about life in new ways, paying close attention to nature and the earth, wondering how to take this new life back into the old one. They laughed in a way few can, for on such journeys our troubles and quirks become obvious. They couldn't hide who they were from one another as they could off the trail, so they had to be willing to accept laughter at their foibles.

They didn't hang on to one another the way people usually do. Hikers have to go their own pace. They did not demand conformity, so letting one another be exactly who they were was the rule, not the exception. In doing so, they moved from group to group, sharing in a common community that was much greater than the small group they resided with for a few days of common pacing. I saw a utopia.

Utopias are great to see, for they can be inspiring, but they are fragile and do not last. Yet on the Appalachian Trail, year after year, pilgrims seek a new way of being. Thousands of men and women have new names, for they have been transformed by a pilgrimage and community that offers this country a different perspective. Maybe someday that community of pilgrims will reach critical mass and spill over into the dominant mass-consumeristic, materialistic culture and we will truly simplify our lives. Because of this unusual lifestyle they were engaging in, more than most of us they understood how much we have, how weighted down we are by what we have, and how little we truly need. They knew that when we need less, we will have less reason to fight and defend ourselves, and we can make our communities into true communities.

The first day I was on the trail helped me see the common rhythm of the hikers. Jonah, who liked to hike at a much faster pace than me, slowed himself down so that we could hike together and talk. We would go on for two to four miles, then sit down to rest. Within a few minutes, his friends would come by, drop their packs, sit, talk, and rest with us. I have been used to short breaks, but we would relax and talk for about an hour before someone would get up to go, then others would stretch and move on as well. There was a common agreement that we would seek to meet at a particular shelter that night, but everyone was aware that Ice Cream might not make it because his trail companion dog was ailing. That was obviously okay with everyone, for they had confidence in two things: Ice Cream knew how to take good care of himself, and he would catch up with them later on the trail. Hiking friends, they told me, come and go.

On the second day of hiking, as we sat on an overlook, Ten Percent said to me, "We've named you 'Dave Thomas'" (the founder of Wendy's restaurants). I laughed, feeling somewhat disappointed that they hadn't come up with a more creative name—because everyone makes fun of my name—but I accepted it, which, I learned later, is necessary for a name to stick. It made me part of the community.

Later that afternoon we met up with a friend of Autumn Leaves who had once hiked the trail himself. He brought us snack foods, beer, and stories. They referred to him as a "trail angel." Trail angels are people who surprise the hikers with unusual generosity or help.

The hikers said that life on the trail has a magic about it—things just work out. Trail angels are a large part of the reason hikes work out so well. Trail angels were part of the watchfulness they all seemed to possess. They were not only looking for and open to good fortune, they named it when they got it.

We left that pleasant magical interlude with about three miles to walk before darkness. Having little time left, we hoofed it pretty quickly, sticking together for the final few miles before rest. At one point I found myself walking near the rear of the group where I encountered in full force what they often laughed about: the smell! We were all so smelly from the sweating and dirt that it was as if walking with a group of wet dogs. They were used to it, of course, having been on the trail for more than two months, but for me it was a shock. I have smelled street people in cities who rivaled the odor, but that is about it. The next day we would pass through a town, go into a restaurant and be asked to sit at the bar, for, the waitress said, "I'm sorry, but no one will eat in the dining room with you there." It wasn't prejudice. It was the smell!

The next morning I watched Autumn Leaves, a small, skinny (bearded) man eat a pot of oatmeal with raisons and nuts that was filled with enough food to feed six normal people. Autumn Leaves had the biggest appetite, but they all ate like horses. It was another thing they had in common and laughed about.

Once during a rest break Stitches was making fun of Autumn Leaves' name. We all agreed it fit, for he was the naturalist among the group, but Stitches said he thought his full name should be "Vernal Swamp Covered with Autumn Leaves." It was so silly that we spent hours laughing with him about his full name. Truly, though, it was a way the group was expressing their full acceptance of Autumn Leaves. They loved his knowledge of the plants and interest in snakes. He would share various greenery for us to taste at nearly every stop.

We spent a night on an overlook on Blue Mountain in Pennsylvania. Jonah and I planned to wake up early to watch the sunrise. As we rose, all of the others quietly rose with us and we all sat in near silence soaking in the majestic change of colors and changing shadows. Something deeply mystical was happening, something that words could not express. A togetherness occurred, too, that was inspiring.

Around a campfire on my last night we talked about the great adventure the hikers were on, about the special relationships they were developing. They had an acceptance of one another, an openness with one another, a willingness to part ways when necessary, and a protectiveness of one another that was quite special. They were not only proud to be part of it, they were awed by its naturalness. It was obviously deeply significant to each person.

After my last night with them, Stitches and Bashful walked back down a short mountain with Jonah and I to meet my ride. They would go on to hike another eighteen miles that day. I would ride and fly back to Memphis, dead tired, but awed by the community experience they had let me into. They had shown me life from a new vista.

What I learned from this view was that communities are partly about journeys that transform us. A level of discipline and common purpose exists in community that draws members into a new way of being. I left the trail with the feeling that these thru-hikers had a grasp of a way of life that offered hope for a friendlier, gentler way of living. In a society overloaded with possessions and stress, they knew how to look for magic. How? They knew that it had to do with carefulness—being full of care—and taking a relaxed but steady pace.

A story is told of a man who bragged to his friends that his wife could do something no other woman could do—carry a full grown cow up one hundred steps. His friends, except for one, wagered with him that she couldn't do it. Going to his hillside home, he told his petite wife it was time to bring the cow up the stairs. Without a word she went down to the pasture below and carried their cow up the one hundred steps to their barn. The man's friends were awed, and asked how she could do such a feat. The husband said that she started carrying the cow up the steps out of love for it when it was but a small calf and had simply never stopped. After the men paid their debt the husband asked his one friend why he hadn't wagered like the others. The man replied, "You were so sure of yourself, I figured she must have been doing it every day."

Two thousand, one hundred and seventy-five miles can be walked only a little bit every day, but it can be done, and it is best done when surrounded by a community. I am convinced that our modern life is most troubled when we lose touch with community. We may live in a neighborhood and call a town "home," but if all we do is stay in our air-conditioned houses with the television on and travel from home to job cubicle in our cars, we don't really know what community is. Isolation breeds habits that harm us. They make us fat, angry, insecure, and wanting more and more.

In contrast, pilgrims on the Appalachian Trail intentionally and intensely wrestle with our way of life. That is their common transcendent vision. Their utopian lives are not feasible to maintain beyond six months, but they exit the trail transformed and still seeking a better way. When they return to our more traditional way of life, they crave what is best from it and try hard not to be swallowed up in isolation and bad habits.

Make no mistake about it—living a life that transcends the debilitating nature of our way of life is up against much, but if Appalachian Trail hikers have anything to give us, it is that some people truly and daily make the effort toward a more meaningful existence. And they reside in community.

Chapter 3

Athletic Community:
Hendrix Cross Country
and Track, 1971-1972

Perhaps my first experience with community independent of my childhood was with my college track and cross country team. It was there that I first began to see the importance of a central "live wire" in community life—a role our coach played. Coach Gerald Cound became, for me, not only a mentor, but also a lifelong friend who helped me see how transformative community can be.

High school athletic teams were great. I loved the comradery, playfulness, and common purpose, but college athletics was different. Grown, mature men are on a college team. They have input into the coach's plan. They are interested in mentoring, and they know that practice is supposed to be both work *and* fun. Thus, they have fun while working hard—very hard. The team I walked onto was composed of such men among us boys.

Coach Cound knew much more and taught in more depth than what I had experienced in high school. He saw in me—a small-time successful runner—someone who was not as good as I thought I was. I knew he appreciated me and my ability, but he kept criticizing my form. One day in practice he outran me to show me he knew what he was talking about. Then he took us to a big-time meet in which I thought I would do well, and I got my comeuppance. Expecting to finish in the top five, I finished sixty-eighth.

My best friend on the team and running partner, Cary Bradburn, was a similarly cocky runner who finished at the back with me and other wanabees. We would take turns setting school records over the next three years, but that first cross country season in 1969 was defi-

doi:10.1300/5653_04

23

nitely a learning experience. It took me most of my first two years to figure out what Coach Cound was trying to help me learn about efficient form—the kind of form that would make me capable of finishing even big races in the top five.

Meanwhile, Coach Cound was teaching others on the team how to be excellent runners, jumpers, and throwers. By the spring of 1972 Coach had assembled a core of good, disciplined athletes. We did not win the conference championship, but our team did better than our small school, Hendrix College, had done for years in the Arkansas Intercollegiate Conference. We did so well that Coach Cound was named AIC Coach of the Year. He told us all, "You did the work. I just watched."

Some teams are just collections of athletes who perform well together—mostly by talent. Some teams perform well together because they enjoy one another and have excellent leadership. These are true teams. In the spring of 1972, our Hendrix College track team was a true team.

What made it different? First of all, we had a coach who understood both humility and leadership. Though barely ten years older than most of us, he accepted the inevitable boundary between coach and team. He was the brunt of most of our ridicule. We made fun of his bald head, his catchphrases, his pep talks, his driving, his physique, his attitude. Nothing was sacred. But we knew he was special. During a time of coach-athlete alienation over dress codes and hair, he let us be ourselves. He accepted our rebelliousness as long as it didn't include laziness or lack of courage. He laughed at our seriousness as much as we laughed at him. What he helped us accept—because he could accept it from us—was that we didn't have all the answers. He taught us to be humble.

Sometimes the wisdom of a teacher can be boiled down to a few phrases. Coach Cound was such a teacher. He used the following three phrases over and over:

1. No matter what the weather, "it's just right."
2. "Don't sweat the small stuff."
3. "Don't stop running now; you're just entering your prime."

He said them so often they became mantras for us all. They gave us a special perspective that helped us become a true team. They were part of our transcendent vision.

THE WEATHER IS JUST RIGHT

At first we hated Coach Cound's idea that no weather was bad weather. As with most runners, we preferred nice days. But he kept saying it, accompanied by his cheerful smile and easy laugh. "Ah, it's just right," he'd say, shaking his head at our complaints. Gradually, we adopted his lead and became enamored with being tough bad-weather runners. Cary came up with a name for us on particularly sloppy days: the "Mud Graphers." We learned to love to practice in downpours and snowstorms. If the weather was bad, we wanted to be in it. Every one of us, as soon as we got outside on a rainy day hit the first mud puddle we saw and got the discomfort of the cold water out of the way. From then on through the rest of our run we were just as interested in getting dirty and wet as we were in working hard.

To this day the main attention I pay to weather is what adventure it will offer me. Yes, I am lazier then I was then, but when I am not making fifty-year-old excuses, I love "bad" weather. It is "just right."

Coach Cound's maxim was about something much more important than the weather. He was teaching us an attitude about life. What if crises were not curses, but good experiences? What if problems were not troubles, but opportunities for something new? What if we really did treat all experiences as "just right"?

I remember the first race of the track season. We traveled to Magnolia, Arkansas, in March to run in a meet on a cool, very windy day. For middle-distance runners, high winds are tough to run in. The disadvantage of running half a lap against the wind more than makes up for the ease of running a half lap with it. Wind disrupts a runner's form and rhythm. Coach Cound, however, by this time had convinced us all that bad weather didn't give anyone an advantage over anyone else. Cary and I were tired, sore, and stiff from those hard early season workouts, frankly, we were both more worried about how we felt than we were about the weather. Yet we had bought into Coach's maxim so well, that we nonchalantly ran along with the lead pack in the race. As far as we were concerned, everything was just right for this time of the year. We stayed relaxed and determined, and in the last 100 yards Cary and I pulled away from the other runners and came in first and second. We thought it was one of the smartest races we had ever run. As I look back it was smart mainly because of our attitude. Despite the handicaps we began with—high winds, soreness, and fatigue—we believed it was just right. When a runner can relax with such an attitude, he or she can run one's best.

As the season went on we found the whole team buying into this attitude. Each meet, each obstacle, each day, any kind of weather, was just right. But we also knew that the other teams in the league were loaded with sometimes twice as many runners as we had, and that because of this we really did not have a chance to win the conference championship. Instead of a losing attitude, though, we relished the idea of having outstanding performances at the conference meet. The final meet before the conference championship, we traveled to Monticello, Arkansas, where our mile relay team, our 440 relay team, our broad and triple jumper, our pole vaulter, and our shot putter all had outstanding performances. Cary and I were first and second in both the mile and the three mile, and I set a school record in the three. We were ready!

At the conference championship meet we knew that we probably couldn't win most of the races we were best at, but we knew we could place better than anyone would expect if we did our best.

Running is primarily an individual sport. Runners are normally very individualistic. We often run alone, and when competing we hardly notice anyone except those right around us, but that day was different. Our team was rooting for one another. We had developed an esprit de corps that meant a great deal to us all. We wanted everyone to run new personal bests.

I have found that personal bests rarely happen in bunches among athletes unless major team support exists. Half the time a runner runs a personal best just because he or she is relaxed. But no one at a championship meet can truly relax. We were not relaxed that day, for we wanted to achieve excellence, to do our best. What we had was team spirit. Early in the meet our 440 relay team, which no one but us expected to place in the top five, came in third and set a school record. Then I ran a school record in placing second in a close mile run. Our pole vaulter came in second. Our triple jumper placed surprisingly high. Then I won the three mile. Finally, our mile relay, never seen by anyone as a strong team, was able to place sixth. As a team we beat three schools that had been favored over us. That was the performance that earned Coach Cound "Coach of the Year." Nearly every performer on the team achieved personal bests.

Yet it was not placing first that made the day. It was doing our best. As one who won an event, I was particularly satisfied with myself, but what I learned about what a team can do was more important to me than my own victory. I had experienced how a team that jells lifts all its members up to higher levels of achievement.

DON'T SWEAT THE SMALL STUFF

Our team was not a well-funded team. When we traveled, if we had to stay overnight, Coach Cound often found us room on the floor of his friends' houses. We slept in tents some nights. We ate in local cafes where the food was cheaper, and our equipment was simple and cheap. Hendrix College just didn't put its money into track and cross country.

It was quite important to us that Coach Cound had a simple philosophy encased in that simple maxim: "Don't sweat the small stuff." I remember him saying to us often, "You don't need anything but shoes and shorts to run. The best thing isn't the equipment, it's the run. Equipment is small stuff." After a few years of looking at other programs that were well funded, receiving perks and carrying the latest equipment and bags, we could have been jealous, but instead we took great pride in being simple athletes who did our best and sometimes even won some races.

Coach's training philosophy was simple, too. He did not believe in the long, laborious practices that other teams had. We ran hard—very hard—with little rest between runs, then practice was over. Once, a competitor from another school told me about his toughest practice. It lasted two hours, and it was one I often did in less than one hour. When he asked about ours and I told him of our ninety-minute practice that included twenty-five quarter-mile runs in under seventy seconds, he was aghast at not only how difficult it was but also at how quickly we did it. I took great pride in our training regiment, and I also always defeated that runner!

Coach Cound used this maxim most often right before meets when we were all nervous. At such times we would want the day to go like clockwork, but life doesn't work that way very often. He'd chuckle and say, "Oh, don't sweat the small stuff. The competition is the big thing." It annoyed us at first . . . until the saying became our own, not just his.

He was teaching us *perspective*. Perspective is defined by Merriam-Webster's as "the capacity to view things in their true relations or relative importance." Coach Cound was helping us understand that many things we worry about, when we back away for a moment and gain perspective—seeing them as part of the whole—are actually small and not nearly as significant as they seem from close up.

I am not one who comes upon being easygoing naturally, yet over the years I've been accused of it. What I think I truly have is Coach Cound's motoo: "don't sweat the small stuff." Funny how a simple saying repeated ad nauseam can become a part of who we are. I was only twenty years old when that simple lesson got into my way of being. It has affected me ever since.

DON'T STOP RUNNING NOW— YOU'RE JUST ENTERING YOUR PRIME

When I entered Hendrix College, Coach Cound was only thirty years old. The summer before he took over the cross country team he got back into competitive shape and ran a series of tight races against the best runner Arkansas had ever had: Jim Crawford. Cound had once won the national Amateur Athletic Union half-mile championship, so he knew what he was doing. He understood not only the mechanics of form, the structure of training, and the tactics of racing, but also the impact of age on a runner. He knew that a runner's prime was in his late twenties. Therefore, all of his athletes were five to ten years away from their physical primes. He kept suggesting to us that we would run much better *after* college.

It became obvious to us very quickly that Coach Cound was teaching a way of life, not a stage of life. He wanted us to learn to put running into *how* we lived life, not just think of it as a temporary diversion or hobby. Not only did he preach such a lifestyle, though, he lived it. He kept in tremendous condition himself. He could work as hard as any man I knew. He was not afraid of any athlete. His physical confidence was incredible to us. Of course we made fun of him—that is what athletes do behind their coaches' backs, but our humor about him was about his great strengths. We especially loved to laugh at him on cold mornings when he was working hard with us and steam would rise off of his bald head.

As with many men with great confidence, Cound laughed at himself as much as we laughed at him. He did not need to defend himself. He knew he was okay. And we knew he was okay, too. He was the type of man we all aspired to be.

Yet Gerald was leaving his physical prime. He was already suffering from arthritis, and he knew that his best competitive years were behind him. He had young children, major responsibilities at Hendrix, and his races with Crawford must have told him something of his growing limitations. At the same time Gerald was moving into another prime: his vocational prime. He was getting his master's in education, his teams were excelling despite a second class athletic environment, and his leadership was being noticed and desired. He would not stop running either, for he was just entering his prime.

He had done it again: his maxim was more metaphorical than literal. Here I am, now in my early fifties, way past my physical prime, but I'm still running, for I'm just entering my prime. Only this prime is about writing and teaching and organizing. The running I'm doing now is enduring the daily grind of writing and reading and thinking and rewriting. But I can't stop now, for I'm just entering my prime!

COMMUNITY MENTORS

I learned from Gerald three simple phrases that have had an inordinate impact on my life. What Gerald really was to me and to most of us on that special team was a mentor. Communities offer mentors to those who are younger.

A natural give and take occurred between Gerald and us athletes. He gave us perspective; we gave him our appreciation. He taught us; we showed him what worked and what didn't. Those being mentored often take what their mentor gives them, and then they take it to the next level. Hegel believed that that is the natural order of life: a thesis or idea is contrasted with antithesis or resistance or a counteridea, which is synthesized into a new and more fully developed idea.

Gerald used to talk with me often about staying relaxed in competition. That was hard for me to do. It is so easy to get tense in one's upper body during the course of a race, especially toward the end of the race. I had trouble with tightening up during most of my first two years at Hendrix. In fact, during my first year I even tightened up during practice, mainly because I ran in practice as if I was racing. I was obsessed with being first, and it was wearing me out and alienating me from my teammates. Somewhere during my second year, however, I made two very important discoveries. First, I discovered that I could run my best when I let me arms move freely, without tension or effort. I had developed good form, so that my arms no longer flew about wildly if I relaxed. I could relax and run free, and I developed an excellent finishing kick. I learned how to run fast when I was dead tired. That made me a formidable competitor with the league's best runners, a position that helped me learn even more about the benefits of competition.

I discovered that the best runners in the league really liked and respected one another. They actually worked together through at least two-thirds of every race. Though the last one-third was "every man for himself," unlike the less experienced runners they were not tense from competing against one another through the bulk of the race. I learned what I earlier referred to: the difference between competing *with* and competing *against*. The best runners competed *with* one another for most of the race, saving themselves for a short period of competing *against* one another. So when they completed a race they thanked one another for the help!

I look back now with amazement at the transformation that took place in my experience with runners. I am convinced that my early motivation for being a good runner was to prove myself, to make myself stand out so much that people would like me. To my chagrin, when I first excelled I discovered that most people admired me from a distance. They saw me as someone obsessed with excellence, someone who belonged in another league from the one that normal people live in. In other words, they viewed me as abnormal. But when I found a new way of competing—one that respected my competitors, shared training secrets, advised one another on ways to do better, one that was as intent upon helping my opponent as beating him—I found community.

I learned that doing one's best is more important than winning. I learned that a race well run is a thing of beauty, not necessarily a victory. Victory is icing in the cake. It is not the cake. I learned all this as a "jock." I learned it on a team that was a community that gave us life.

Chapter 4

Mark Class

I found many mentors at Hendrix College, but it was not until my first year of seminary that I experienced an academic class that functioned as a community in the same way our track team, as described in Chapter 3, did.

Professor Walter Wink is a well-known biblical theologian and social interpreter. When I was a student at Union Theological Seminary in New York City, he was a young associate professor seeking to gain full professorship at Union. He had just published a book titled *The Bible in Human Transformation* (Wink, 1973). In that book he asserted that the Bible is a book intended to change people, and, read from that perspective, one must ask questions that encourage transformation. He used Jungian theory, psychological techniques, and biblical criticism and scholarship to help students discern what the biblical writer and biblical stories meant to students *personally*. His most important class at Union was his "Mark" class—a semester course on the Gospel of Mark for a limited number of students. The reason enrollment in the class was limited was because he asked all students to share personal reflections on each text being studied. It was not a class for one who did not want to be self-disclosing. Students had to share in this transcendent vision so that we could understand the Gospel of Mark on a *personal* level.

At that time in my life I was struggling with many personal changes, which had led me to seek the personal help of a pastoral counselor. I craved sharing and wanted very much to be a part of Walter's class, and spending some time on the waiting list until finally being accepted into the class.

Most professors of biblical studies at Union in those days (the mid-1970s) subscribed to a triangular approach to studying the Bible. In

doi:10.1300/5653_05

different styles and forms they would say "There are the text, the context, and you." Our Mark class followed a discussion format based on that triangle. We would carefully read the text, inspecting translations, possible editorial changes, comparing different accounts and different word usage between the synoptic gospels (Matthew, Mark, and Luke). Then we would study the context: When was it written? What exactly was happening during the time of the story? Where exactly was it? Finally, Walter would ask us a series of questions that would take us inside the text itself: Who do you identify with? Why? Is what's going on today similar to what was happening then? Why? How are you similar to the different characters in the story, especially the antagonists? What does the text say to you today? Why?

Sometimes it was tough work, eliciting tears. Walter was pushing us to encounter the text in ways that opened us up, pushed us to change. He did it by asking simple questions, sometimes so simple that the answer was self-evident (such as, "Who were the main characters in the story?"), then sitting quietly and patiently for someone to respond. He would tell us that it was important to ask a question, even dumb ones, with authority and humility, then wait, and he was an example of that confidence. Eventually we began to follow his style. We learned to sit comfortably with the silence and look carefully for a genuine response. Walter also taught us to receive all responses with grace and warmth.

During the semester I was in his class Walter was being considered for tenure at the seminary. A great amount of work is involved in the tenure process, including rigorous examination of one's publications, one's promise, one's teaching ability, and one's work ethic. Although Walter was one of the most popular teachers at Union, he was denied tenure. We heard that he was told that he was not scholarly enough. It was a major disappointment for us students.

Toward the end of the semester we gathered for a retreat at the Fellowship of Reconciliation center in Nyack, New York. We studied some of the more dramatic stories from Mark in great depth there. What I remember most, however, is how we did it. Walter's wife, Virginia, was a dancer and bioenergetics therapist. She asked us to move with her in ways that might open up our emotions. We tensed up then released the tension, moved in angry ways, found postures of despair and pain. It was very evocative. Walter joined us—the first time I had

had a professor join in with students in the student's humble position. We then studied the story often referred to as "The Healing of the Paralytic." In this story (Mark 2:1-12), Jesus is teaching in a crowded home, when some friends of a paralyzed man bring him to the home in hopes of getting Jesus to heal him. Because of overcrowding, they are turned away at the door, so they climb onto the home's roof and create an opening, then lower the man down through the opening to where Jesus is teaching. Based on this act of faith, Jesus tells the paralyzed man that his sins are forgiven. After some outrage from the people present who question Jesus' authority to forgive sins, Jesus tells the paralyzed man that his faith has made him well, and orders him to get up and walk. The man does, to everyone's amazement. After our usual manner of studying the text, the question that most captivated our class was "How are you paralyzed now?" Walter gave us hunks of clay and asked us to create a sculpture that would express our own personal paralysis. An hour later we returned to the group, and nearly everyone, including Walter, shared very personal stories connected with their sculptures. It was deeply moving.

Walter shared a sculpture that was particularly important for our class, for it was deeply personal and confessional, which was not the normal professional behavior. He had sculpted a bird's wing with an arrow lodged in it. He said, "This is how I feel after being denied tenure—as if I now have a wounded wing and can't fly."

Here was a man who had taught a class that was deeply transforming for many of us. He had given us insights not only into the Bible, into how to teach, but also into our own souls, and he was still willing to be as vulnerable as we were. I had never in my life experienced such a leader. Leaders, in my experience, stayed aloof. They did not humble themselves and share their deepest pain and fears. Walter was giving me a new view of leadership. It was inspirational to me.

It was my first encounter with a broadened view of leadership that included vulnerability. Walter was, indeed, the live wire of that group, but not just because of his position and abilities; it was also because he was willing to be present with his students at our level. Students are naturally in a humble position, and few teachers, in my experience, are willing to join them at that level. When Walter joined us in dance and sculpture he set a tone for a deeper level of openness.

One of the main characteristics of the live wire who sparks community feeling is openness. The courage to be vulnerable and visible

is the key to offsetting the narcissistic element of the live wire position in a group. Narcissism itself has a dividing line between pleas-
antness and oppressiveness. Pleasant narcissism is entertaining—the
word *outgoing* most captures this idea. Oppressive narcissism is domi-
neering and sometimes even evil. What keeps us on the pleasant side
is the humility that accompanies openness and vulnerability. Walter
was such a person. As a teacher in a prestigious graduate school, he
had to have had the ego to seek such a position. It definitely had its
narcissistic reinforcements, but he accompanied that narcissistic
temptation with a willingness to join us students in our humble position. His wounded bird was a picture of wounded narcissism, but it
was also a universal image of human woundedness. Is there a conscious human soul that does not know what it feels like to be shot
down in "flight"? When we are beginning to soar, don't we all know
the experience of being grounded, pulled back to earth?

Walter had, in being vulnerable and open with us, created an image
that added to the potential depth of our developing community. It was
that image that has stayed with me as representative of what the Mark
class community experience was truly about.

Memories of community experiences are compressed into images,
embodied in symbolic events. Walter's shared sculpture, a universal
image, captured my imagination for years and reminded me of what
we experienced that semester at Union. More important, some of
Walter's vulnerability and humility was internalized in me, despite
my own narcissism. After that community experience, I would never
again be able to view leadership the same. Before that class I had seen
leadership as something done from above, aloof from the common
folks. After the Mark class I knew that leadership for community is
different. Leadership in community (or *for* community) reaches out
vulnerably, openly, and humbly. That one class became more than a
class. It changed many of us—certainly it did me. It was a community
that gave us life.

Chapter 5

In His Steps

In 1896 Charles Shelton, the pastor at Central Congregational Church in Topeka, Kansas, preached a series of story-sermons about a pastor in a Midwestern city who asked his congregation to

> pledge themselves, earnestly and honestly for an entire year, not to do anything without first asking the question, "What would Jesus do?" And after asking that question, each one will follow Jesus as exactly as he knows how, no matter what the result may be. (Shelton, 1935, p. 15)

He published the sermons in a religious weekly, the *Chicago Advance,* then they were published in the book, *In His Steps: "What Would Jesus Do?"* as a public domain paperback. It became a best seller, a major example of the social gospel movement in the early twentieth century.

I read my mother's copy of the book published in 1935 when I was fifteen years old. Deeply stirred by the book, I wondered what it would be like to actually live with that question before me. I thought, probably rightfully so, that I would be ostracized from my friends—not a fate I desired—but I was so moved by the book and the idea that I felt the need to respond with some degree of honesty and integrity. In that state of inspiration, I said to myself and vowed to God that "When I become an adult I will ask 'What would Jesus do?' before everything I do." Then I forgot about the vow and lived the usual life of a teenager—until I was seventeen and listening to the baccalaureate sermon at my high school graduation. The preacher kept saying that we were now adults. At that moment I decided to live by Shelton's vow.

doi:10.1300/5653_06

Of course, at that age one is not fully conscious of what he or she is doing, so, despite trying to live by a new standard for decision-making, I basically followed the script for a southern white boy. I went to college, participated in athletics, dated, explored around, and tried to fulfill my personal obligations. One day during my junior year I was invited to participate in a dorm "beer bust" to be held off campus on a beach on the Arkansas River. I was told that it was being secretly paid for by the dorm's activity fees. In other words, it was not only illegal, it was being hidden from the school's administration. Although I am not nor was I then opposed to drinking in moderation, I was very disturbed by this. To go along with it would be to condone not only excessive drinking and secretive usage of school funds, but also, and especially, drunk driving. I felt that Jesus would do something about it, even in the face of peer pressure. So I told the dorm president that I would not go along with the beer bust and why. He said, "Well, you don't have to go along. We'll do it without you." I replied, "No, I mean you can't use dorm money for it. If you try to, I will inform the dean of students." I did have to inform the dean of students, and the beer bust was canceled. Many of the dorm residents were not happy with me. But I felt a strange and strong sense of rightness. I had stopped something that I still feel would have been irresponsible and immoral.

What I didn't have, though, was something that has become more evident to me over the years, something that is described in Shelton's book. In *In His Steps,* after the pastor of Shelton's fictitious town of Raymond's First Church, Henry Maxwell, had issued his challenge to the congregation to follow in Jesus' steps for a year. Some congregants took immediate actions that appeared impulsive (such as the city's newspaper editor refusing to report on certain sports events). In the beginning little consultation or shared prayer occurred. As the story progressed, however, the depth of thought and clarity of ideas grew significantly. It grew in dialogue and prayer. Early decisions were made by individuals with strong ideas about morality, but later decisions grew out of moral considerations that had been considered and refined in the community. Shelton describes special gatherings to discuss their commitments and decisions, meetings that were filled with spiritual power and rich dialogue. Unusually strong bonds were also formed between people who had been merely social friends.

In fact, halfway into the story the focus for decision making expanded from the simple question "What would Jesus do?" to a broader, more complex statement: "seek first the Kingdom of God." With that shift, a clear movement was made from individualism to community. Now the community was the staging ground for major decisions in individuals' lives. People had begun to make decisions in dialogue with their friends, and not just because they thought it was something Jesus would do.

When I was in my early twenties I did not see such an aspect of change. I was still wrapped up in how my individual conscience could be an adequate gauge for judging what Jesus would or would not do. Although I still think what I did about the beer bust was the right thing to do, without a community surrounding me in my attempt to follow in Jesus' steps my only source of interpretation was just me, which was subject to great fallacy.

A couple of years later I got married. My wife, from whom I could not hide some aspects of myself, did not believe that I was as pious as I led myself to believe. She got tired of my assertion that I made my decisions based on what Jesus would do. She saw me as self-righteous and would argue vehemently with me. I didn't think Jesus would be argumentative, yet I was reactively argumentative with my wife, so I found myself unable to live by my own ideals. In addition, I could not justify the anger I felt. Jesus, I thought, wouldn't have had my temper. I was disturbed with myself, angry at my wife (who dared to challenge my piety), and I felt guilty.

One day I sat down and wrote this essay:

> There is a serious human inadequacy that is prematurely and passively accepted in the ethical ideal of *In His Steps*. It does not deal realistically with the self: What should *I* do? It tends to substitute an often ambiguous and unclear Jesus for inexperience and shortcomings while using subjective feelings to define the clarity of the ethical standard. In other words, it places justification on the "follower" more so than responsibility, because his feelings will be superimposed over the ambiguity of a situation. It is taking an undefined ideal and defining it with one's subjective feelings—which is ethically both inadequate and dangerous.
>
> Probably the greatest danger involved in this standard is the righteousness that the disciplined and justified feelings gain because of their "fulfillment." Since its benefits are "good feelings," the stress of ethical activity is reduced or even eliminated,

thereby making the "follower" feel as if he or she is reaching a level of "holiness" or "righteousness" that is unassailable or irreproachable. Regardless of his or her outward expressions of tolerance, flexibility, and acceptance of others, this person tends to feel that because he or she feels so good everyone else would be that much better off if they too would adopt this ethical standard. He or she feels that everyone should feel as good and could if they would adopt it. He or she is a paragon of that standard and others should follow it also. Not only is it the way to righteousness, it is perceived as the right way for others to feel happy. In a way, he or she feels a special calling to actually control this lofty, holy ideal.

I have been guilty of this righteousness. I cannot, of course, say "go away" and it will all vanish, but I think that in this recognition and confession I can deal with challenging my ethics on a thoughtful and productive level. This calls so much of my righteousness into question, sometimes even unjustifies my behavior. I am challenged to search anew for deeper ethical standards.

Upon completion of the essay I immediately felt as if I had no ethical standard anymore. I felt as if I was now living in an "ethical vacuum." What it really took away from me was hubris. In writing the essay I was admitting that I had developed a self-righteousness that kept me apart from community. I may have lost my sense of ethics, temporarily, but I was no longer judgmental enough to exclude myself from community. What I now was free to learn was that community leads one to better ethics—which is just what Charles Shelton was showing as his story progressed.

In the latter chapters of the book, Shelton (1935), through the preaching voice of Reverend Maxwell, asks, "What [is] the trouble with the world? It [is] suffering from selfishness" (p. 225). "Nothing but a discipleship of this kind [imitation of Jesus] can face the destructive selfishness of the age with any hope of overcoming it" (p. 239). At this point in Shelton's narrative, and after each of his sermons on the imitation of Jesus, it would appear that the individual is left to decide for himself or herself what is the right way to follow in His steps. But, instead, Shelton always follows such expository with a gathering of community, saying members

came forward, as so many of the church members had done in the morning, and seriously, solemnly, tenderly, took the pledge to do as Jesus would do. A deep wave of spiritual baptism broke over the meeting near its close that was indescribable in its tender, joyful, sympathetic results. (p. 241)

So despite Shelton's warning that the imitation of Jesus leads to suffering, his description of community is not a picture of suffering, but of joy and love—life together, *real* Life.

What I had misunderstood as a young man was not that following in Jesus' steps was inadequate and unjustified, but that the inclination to act in accordance with any ideal is inadequate *unless tempered and refined through community experience*. In the experience of community, one finds wisdom, not just inclination and shallow impulse.

It is important to remember as well Shelton's assertion that the imitation of Jesus leads to suffering, for the love that Jesus calls for in his disciples is filled with compassion for suffering.

If our definition of being a Christian is simply to enjoy the privileges of worship, be generous at no expense to ourselves, have a good, easy time surrounded by pleasant friends and by comfortable things, live respectably and at the same time avoid the world's great stress of sin and trouble because it is too much pain to bear it—if this is our definition of Christianity, surely we are a long way from following the steps of Him who trod the way with groans and tears and sobs of anguish for a lost humanity; who sweat, as it were, great drops of blood, who cried out on the upreared cross, "My God, my God, why hast thou forsaken me?" (Shelton, 1935, pp. 239-240)

In other words, it leads one to minister where suffering is greatest, where bad things happen.

Communities are by their very nature open and inclusive. M. Scott Peck (1980) is correct in saying that when a group shifts to community it does so because some in the group are willing to share their real, human, imperfect selves to the group. They are willing to risk being vulnerable. They are willing to risk suffering. When others, in response, join in that vulnerability and openness, community happens, and when a community forms out of such openness, how can it then be closed and exclusive to others? It can't. If it is closed, it's not really a community—it's a pseudocommunity.

But a problem exists: How can a true community, which by its nature is small enough for its members to share deeply and freely *and* be attractive to many, continue to grow and still hang on to its communal spirit? In other words, does a maximum number of members exist that a community cannot grow beyond and still be a community?

Shelton ends his book with a vision of a great movement in Christendom based upon this radical pledge to do what Jesus would do regardless of the personal consequences. It is a grand and massive vision. It would include millions of people. Is it possible to sustain such a grand vision, to create a megachurch comprised of people who are truly committed to a radical ideal? In the United States, we think so. In this country we live by the notion that "bigger is better." I address this notion in Chapter 6.

Chapter 6

Community and the Church Health Center

I have been involved in some organizations that were so special, so dynamic, that they changed me. From them I learned organizational skills, how to lead, conflict resolution, and many other skills that have made me into a much better person. The Church Health Center in Memphis, Tennessee, is one such organization. It was different from some of the larger organizations I've participated in. At first it was small. At first it was clearly a ministry of love. It was also so dynamic and magnetic that it grew rapidly into a large organization—at least compared to what it was when I first joined it. That extraordinary growth makes it a good example of the dynamics of growth and what rapid growth does to community life.

In 1987 Dr. Scott Morris, a United Methodist minister and family physician, started a primary care medical clinic for the working poor who cannot afford insurance in Memphis. Scott's initial vision, captured in the center's mission statement was to "reclaim the Church's historical and biblical commitment to care for the poor who are sick." His vision to offer a way for people of faith to care for those less fortunate was captivating to the community. What began with him practicing primary medical care quickly grew to include dentistry, counseling, optometry, health education, exercise and recovery programs, and physical therapy—a full-service medical clinic. In addition, nearly every specialist in Memphis was enlisted to volunteer to serve patients in need of their service (for free!). Even hospitals gave their service to patients of the Church Health Center.

I was one of those captivated by this dynamic ministry. I began volunteering my counseling time and donating money to the center in 1987. What I found was a place where the spirit of the staff was as

doi:10.1300/5653_07

41

extraordinary as the nearly unlimited number of volunteers. Cynically, I thought it couldn't really be this good. I figured they put on their best face for me, a volunteer.

In 1994 I was in a position to join the staff, so I paid them a visit. What I found astounded me. Try as I did, I could find no one who was disgruntled and would complain about how the center operated, other than some minor concerns. This was despite the substantial cuts in salary all the professional staff had taken to work there. They were there for reasons beyond money, and declared that they were truly happy. It was as if I had stumbled onto a perfect workplace. If I had not known many on the staff from my years as a volunteer and therefore knew they were not crazy or brainwashed, I would not have believed it. I could not ignore this common unity of conviction. I took the job and a cut in pay.

On my first day on the job we met with a diverse group of Christian and Jewish leaders to discuss a way to expand what we understood our purpose to be, from just bandaging the wounded to creating a way to stop the wounding. We weren't sure what we were to do, but Scott was initiating a brain trust to see what we would figure out.

Julia Hicks, our health educator, and I became the primary coordinators of the brainstorming. Every week a group of three to seven people would meet in my office and share ideas about how to create a way to help people live healthier lives—healthier on many levels: physically, mentally, spiritually, and socially. Julia and I would draft and redraft proposals. Most of them were scrapped, some turned into experiments or trial gatherings, and a few grew into the eventual idea that drove us forward—the creation of the Hope and Healing Center, a multimillion dollar, multidimensional health and recovery center for people to learn to live healthier lives. Today the Hope and Healing Center in Memphis is a local landmark, one of those places that is always in the news with stories of people finding new life and renewed health. Someday it may be a centerpiece of the nation's movement toward "preventive health care."

When I joined the staff of the Church Health Center we had forty-two employees. Every week we met in two adjoining rooms in the Health Education building for about thirty minutes. At that meeting very brief reports on special projects were given, moments of surprise when someone would tell of an experience with a patient were usually accompanied by moments of levity and laughter, and we would end the meeting with Scott telling a story and giving a theological interpretation of an experience he or someone had had with a patient, then a short prayer. During Advent I would read a portion of the Advent story and tell a Christmas story.

As with all professionals I have been in meetings all of my life. Some of them have been good, but the vast majority of meetings are some variation of what I imagine hell could be like. I have learned to tolerate meetings and have even learned how to make the most of them, and I sometimes even participate in a good meeting. Basically, I've learned that the shorter they are the better, so from the outset I was quite impressed that we had only thirty minute meetings at the Church Health Center.

The meetings were not short just because it was the smart thing to do. They were short, I came to understand, because we were all very aware of what one another was up to. We were carrying the mission of the Church Health Center *as a community*. Ideas and activities were shared through the informal and affectionate channels of the relationships within the community. I knew that Julia talked with Scott, Pat, and Jean almost every day. Julia knew that I talked with Mary Nell, Wendy, and Janice. We knew that Janice talked with Addison, Debbie, Brenda, and Laletta; Debbie with Butch and Kim; and Brenda talked with everybody! It wasn't gossip, though. It was sharing—we were mutually interested in one another and our common work and mission.

We had an enormous amount of people coming to us for help. Most of our days were spent ministering to those who were sick, distressed, or seeking to recover from illnesses. Whenever no-shows or cancellations occurred. During those times we would work on our dreams. In some ways we counted on unpredictable spaces in our days so that we could work together.

And, oh, the dreams! Every day we were free to play with our dreams of how to help people in new and more creative ways. Nobody was getting swallowed up in the nearly overwhelming problems that our poverty-stricken patients were struggling with. Why were we not? It was because the community lifted us up from the despair that we were so close to. Besides the wonderful friendships we had, I think our greatest assets were our dreams. We had time and made space nearly every day to dream dreams. The community had a vision that was captivating to us all.

Much of that vision was from the dynamic leadership of Scott. Scott was great at taking the kernels of ideas from us all and pulling it into the grander vision that he was orchestrating. The very first day I was there I got a taste of it. When Scott asked if one central and simple idea existed that could change people's lives, I offhandedly suggested "walk and talk." We spent hours exploring the value of walking and talking, and, for a while, the experimental name of our imaginary healing center was "Walk and Talk." Later the name became "Healthy Congregations," then "Fit for Service," and eventually someone came up with "Hope and Healing"—which stuck.

Something is truly special about how dreams enhance community. Dreams come, of course, in two forms: imagination dreams (daydreams, nighttime dreams, and captivating stories) and dreams or visions of a better world. Interestingly, both forms of dreams are keys to the creation of community.

I led two groups at the Church Health Center that I called a "Dream Therapy Group." In these groups of five to seven people I encouraged members to share their nighttime dreams with one another so that we could analyze them together. I created the first group on a lark, but was amazed from the start at how quickly the group became a community. Sharing dreams was an immediate doorway into the soul of another. Sharing a dream is an act of vulnerability and openness that draws people together.

The dreams of a better world that we were sharing with one another at the Church Health Center had the same effect. When a person shares such a dream, he or she is sharing an aspect of the self that is filled with soul, filled with hope, and loaded with passion. We could not listen to one another without fascination. This was in spite of the fact that our dreams were usually only pieces of the eventual picture of what we were seeking together.

Every year I would lead the staff retreat in late September. For the first couple of years our retreats were for the purpose of renewal, and the way we did that was to rename what we were about. Our favorite activity was the creation of skits. The most fun was when we created a truly awful clinic with discounting, lazy workers and contrasted that hilarious misadventure with what it should look like. It is almost always funny to see how good people are at imagining how bad they can act!

In 1998 I changed the retreat program to something that we played with for the next five years. Because we had become an organization with nearly eighty people by that time, I had us wrestle with the dynamics of growth. The question I was concerned about was how to maintain a community past a certain number of members. I felt instinctively that our community was threatened by our numbers. By that time we were building the Hope and Healing Center on two fronts: the construction site itself and the preparative programs that would be part of the new space. For years our clinic had been the focus of our growth. We had added new doctors, more dentistry, more volunteer counselors and psychiatrists, a walk-in clinic, and more health education programs. But all this growth had been on the same campus. Now we were adding a whole new dimension and a whole new campus. Computers were upgraded, new directors were appointed, fund-raising grew in importance.

Somewhere between when our numbers were eighty employees and one hundred employees, we changed. Committees began to take on the role of the community. For nearly fifteen years the vision and mission of the center had been lifted up by Scott and the community. Now the community was dying, leaving committees to do the work of lifting up the Center's vision and mission.

Certainly remnants of community could still be seen. In fact, pockets of community existed, but these small groups of cherished friends would no longer just talk about their dreams. Now we also talked about the "good ole days" when everyone knew everyone. An element of grief existed.

Simultaneously another element of our life together gained importance—paperwork, rules, and regulations. In a medical clinic, paperwork is important from the outset. Doctors and support staff must keep careful and accurate records, but our paperwork was being driven by something beyond the community. Communities police themselves, but when a community grows beyond a certain capacity, policing must be more objective. That is what was happening to us.

W. T. Jones (1952), in his work on the history of Western philosophy, had some important insights that shed light on what was happening at the Church Health Center. Writing about the institutionalization of Christianity, they say,

> Movements tend to be radical and extreme. As they are institutionalized, they become conservative and resist the very excitement

and ferment that gave them birth. This is almost inevitable. An institution constitutes a lot of men; rules are needed to reduce the number of separate decisions that are made and so to minimize the changes of contradictory policies' being initiated in different parts of the organization. But the rules are perforce designed for the general case, and since all actual cases are particular, the rule never exactly fits. (pp. 55-56)

We were becoming an institution.

That is not necessarily bad, though. Institutions can get more done, serve more people. They have more power to create change. As I look back, it was on the day that I began work at the Church Health Center that the process toward institutionalization was set in motion. On that day we began to work on a vision of how we could change the way people lived. Up until then our mission was to help individuals. On that day in 1994 when we set about to change society, we began a task larger than what a community can do. We needed power, and power has much to do with numbers.

For me and for many of us who participated in the early community life, however, it was painful, for as the institution rose, the original community died. We grieved. To some extent we all felt that the community would lead to a larger end, but those on the ground floor of a community naturally miss the priority of relationships over rules that becomes reversed when the community gets subsumed by institutionalization.

The Church Health Center is a light not only to the city of Memphis, but it is fast becoming a light to the nation. It offers an alternative method of medical care, as well as a blueprint for helping average Americans live holistically healthier lives. Lifestyle changes might be relatively easy for wealthy, somewhat leisurely oriented people, but the average American does not have that advantage. The Church Health Center and the Hope and Healing Center are terrific places where true hope and deep healing are offered.

It was a community that got the centers going. It is programs and committees that keep them going. Is this a problem? For those who grieve the death of the community, yes. For those who want it to change the way our society lives, no. The community changed the way some of us lived. The institution might change the way our society lives.

Part of the magnetism of community is what kills it. Communities such as the Church Health Center draw people and resources to it in the same way a magnet attracts iron. Because of that magnetism, we grew naturally and steadily, until, one day we reached the point of critical mass in which the organization had to become an institution. As Jones and Fogelin said, it was inevitable.

What I still struggle with, though, is whether or not the Church Health Center, which is now much, much bigger and powerful, is truly better. Is bigger better? In America we normally think so, but I am not sure it is. In fact, sometimes I think bigger is definitely not better. Even in the case of excellent institutions such as the Church Health Center and other such idealistic organizations or ministries, I am not sure. I can see their power and influence spreading far and wide, changing people and our way of life in ways that a small community does only for a select few. But is it really better? Does an institution really change the structure of the way things are, or does it just rearrange our functions?

Some interesting phenomena shed light on these questions. Communities have throughout history lasted only relatively short periods of time but have had an enormous influence on the world around them. One of the first was the community that surrounded Socrates. A small group of radical thinkers, these Greek men wrestled with the deepest problems of the universe, and after Socrates' courageous death, kept asking questions and lifting up new theories that continue to influence us today. Jesus was surrounded by a small community of disciples that, after Jesus' death, changed the world. Saint Francis of Assisi surrounded himself with a community of radical priests who changed Catholicism. European philosophical circles during the eighteenth and nineteenth centuries were incredibly dialogical and rich with ideas that have had enormous influence on the world. The revolutionary community of the early United States created maybe the greatest political constitution ever created. Martin Luther King Jr. was surrounded by a community whose members, after his death, entered politics and transformed the face of American government.

Communities, though they split apart and die, give birth to greatness. I think that every great person has been touched by some community experience. As I watch what has happened to those who were fortunate enough to be part of the early Church Health Center but now have moved on to other places as successful doctors, nurses, church workers, and professionals. The sphere of influence of that community is astounding in a way. I would be shocked if it attains anything close to the historical movements I cited previously, but nearly all of us are functioning at a higher level than we were before we experienced life together. Communities may die, but the spirit of the community is resurrected in the transformed lives of those who move on from the community springboard. Communities make people better.

Yet, despite my questions, communities still are nurtured even in the largest of institutions. One of the most common comments about so-called "megachurches" is "It's large, but it seems small." For within the well-organized megachurch are many small communities, usually Sunday school classes. The best functioning large organizations inevitably are comprised of small community cells that lift up pieces of the mission of the whole. In fact, now at the Church Health Center are small group meetings with this very intent. They are attempting to give employees opportunities to form communities that might make the whole organization better. Furthermore, as a friend of mine once said, "In spite of the conservatism of the large institution, good ideas are still occasionally smuggled in." I believe that these "good ideas" come primarily out of community life. An individual might give birth to it, but the community raises it and "smuggles" it into institutional life.

Not so many self-contained communities exist within our massive societies today, but communities still exist within the institutions. It is my assertion that the vitality of those communities is crucial to the sustenance of the life of those institutions and even to the health of the larger society.

Chapter 7

Memphis Friends Meeting

What happens when a community intentionally limits its growth? Does it therefore limit the good it can do? I do not know the answer, but my experience with the Memphis Friends Meeting sheds some light on these questions.

Enter an unprogrammed Quaker meeting for worship and you will see a diverse group of people sitting in a circle of meditative silence. Some will be dressed up, most will be dressed casually. You will receive eye contact from a few, welcoming nods and smiles, but that is all. It might feel as if nothing is happening, for it is so quiet and still. Stomachs growl and no one apologizes for them, chairs might creak as some shift their positions, but no one pays much attention. Occasionally a parent might whisper to his or her fidgeting child. You might wonder how they can take all the silence. However, a relaxed comfort is about the room. Usually the silence lasts and lasts. At first it's unnerving, then it's relaxing. Some stare blankly ahead, some look about the room, some sit with eyes closed, and someone usually nods a bit, obviously half dozing. Some of the children leave along with a couple of adults. You missed the signal that gave them permission to move, but it's done so smoothly and quietly, you are surprised. They go into another room and you can hear their muffled voices and activities, but it's not really disturbing. In fact, none of the noises around you are troublesome. You hear things usually unheard: traffic going by outside, birds singing, a city bus, people walking by on the sidewalk. You see the shadows from the sun moving slowly, or the movement of seated people's dangling feet, bouncing slightly as their hearts beat. You have truly quieted down.

Then someone speaks. It is a simple message, usually something personal followed by some brief thoughts. Some in the room look at

doi:10.1300/5653_08

the speaker. Others don't even move or open their eyes. The silence returns. Sometimes the speaker shakes after speaking, for what he or she shared was so deeply felt. (This shaking is one reason they were named Quakers—the speaker was quaking.) An even deeper stillness and quiet set in now. You can not pinpoint it, but it is as if those gathered have really, really listened to what the speaker said. Another ten minutes of silence goes by, but this time it flies by.

Someone else speaks. This message takes up the theme shared by the first speaker, turns to another insight, and also is short and received with silence and slight gestures of acceptance. Silence returns, then another speaker, who says something so warm and clear that the other two messages seem completed. You feel excited to have witnessed such a spontaneous, complete, insightful message. The simplicity and clarity is awesome. You want to sing, but the silence is so deep you sit aware of your breathing, your contentment, and gratitude.

Children come back into the meeting room and immediately settle into their parents' laps or sit alone in silence. You're impressed with how quiet the children are. There's at least one who is having a hard time of it, but few seem distracted.

An hour has gone by. The first thirty minutes were slow, but the last half hour has gone so quickly you're shocked when you glance at your watch. Suddenly a person in the room offers a hand to a person, and all around the room people are shaking hands and saying hello. The leader of the meeting then leads the group through introductions and announcements. Announcements are about two things: a quaint and curious request to "hold in the Light" some person who is facing a trial, and various organizational and activist announcements. Laughter occurs as well as a quiet acceptance of various concerns. It's as though the group is giving worshipful, silent space between announcements. Children are more active now, but adults are touching them all over the room.

A patient ease is finally accented with a silent pause, and the leader says, "Let's rise." People then stand up and the noise that was missing for that luxurious hour is back. People want to meet you. Others are talking with their friends in twos and threes. Nobody is in a hurry, but gradually the place clears out, you leave, noticing that someone is still there, obviously in charge of locking up.

Such is the traditional Quaker meeting for worship, which are called "unprogrammed," because only two set rituals are practiced:

friends gather in a circle of silence, and the meeting is closed with handshakes. No set program is followed, so almost anything can happen. Some expressions used to be taboo, such as singing or dancing, but today those are even acceptable. Many meetings now include a singing or musical message, and I have seen dance in meetings as well. The reason is because over time Quakers have discovered that the revelation of God cannot be exclusive. It can come from any person in any form. What Quakers seek to do is to discern the messages of the Spirit regardless of the median of expression.

I became a Quaker in 1979 on the heels of a couple of very personal events in my life. First, after graduating from a very liberal seminary in 1977 I had found the typically patriotic and conservative theologies of common churches to be disturbing. In seminary my thinking had been shaped by black liberation theology and other polemics toward our American way of life—particularly the racism, classism, materialism, and militarism. This point of view made me want to see a revolution of values. Mainline protestant churches typically did not share my reformist zeal. I simply could not find comfort in traditional churches. I visited Congregational, United Methodist, Presbyterian, African Methodist Episcopal, African Methodist Episcopal Zion, and Unitarian, but none of them spoke to me. In fact, mostly I returned from visiting churches angry. My wife would ask me, "Why do you visit churches if you come home angry?" I thought that was a good question, so I stopped attending churches. Yet I still felt a pull to find a spiritual home.

One day I decided to visit a Quaker meeting, saying to myself, "I'm going to go to a place where they don't say anything so nothing will upset me!" But between that decision and actually attending a Quaker meeting, another formational event in my life happened. My wife gave birth to our first son. So moved was I by this event, so awed by the newfound love I felt, that by the time I did attend that first Quaker meeting I was more open and less angry at life than I had been in years. Perhaps I could have found peace in any church with this new attitude, but I still think the silence was especially important to me. I had so much noise inside of me that I think I desperately needed the quietness. But the worship was not entirely quiet. The messages truly touched me, or as Quakers say, "spoke to my condition." Even the announcements afterward—which I have come to understand are part of the worship—were helpful to me. I was meeting a group of people who shared my disillusionment with the wasteful, militaristic, exclusive aspects of our way of life, but were finding in their communities ways to confront what they disliked. I not only needed the quietness; I also needed the positive activism. I believe I joined the Quakers that very first meeting for worship. I knew even then that I had found a spiritual home for myself.

Six years later my family and I moved to Memphis, Tennessee. We found a small Quaker worship group meeting at Rhodes College. It was so hidden it took us two months to find it, and when we finally visited, my family of four doubled the worship group's numbers. Within two months we organized ourselves into a traditional Quaker structure and grew from the original four attenders to around twenty-five each Sunday. Gradually we found in our group some deeply dedicated individuals who began to create a community that would become an official monthly meeting in 1988, and become a solid and visible presence in Memphis. More important, we would become an important part of one another's lives.

As I look back on the development of our Quaker community I can see various stages of development. The first one was an early immersion and interest in Quaker faith and practice. Together we were learning how to speak out of the silence of worship, finding the courage and inspiration to speak spontaneously, without notes, and with conviction and humility. We were learning the balance between sharing messages and letting silence reign. We were also becoming acquainted and enamored with many of the quaint Quaker sayings, phrases such as "held in the Light," "that of God within," "sit quietly and wait for the way to open," "threshing our conflicts," "finding unity," "the Inner Light." We found ourselves playing with naming all of our gatherings "Meetings for. . . ." We developed a meeting for learning, a meeting for business, and a meeting for worship. We had a meeting for eating. In my own home our youngest son named the blessing before meals our "meeting." It was clear to us that this word was about the connections we were developing with one another. We were meeting "that of God" within each person.

Quaker practices are often hard for children. The quiet and stillness is often more adult oriented than children can stand. Assimilating children into the life of the meeting is important. We found a few ways to honor children and give them a central place in our lives together. First, we always accepted them in meeting for worship for as long as they wanted to stay. Most children would leave for "First Day School" after about ten minutes of worship with the volunteer adult teachers. There they would have playful and instructive activities until the last few minutes of worship when they would return. We often encouraged adults to share messages for the children during those ten minutes. When they returned, sometimes someone would share a brief message for the children that explained what had happened in worship while the children were away. Three of our children began a practice at close of worship that carried on for years. They shook hands with everyone in the circle while we shared announcements. We called them our "welcoming committee." Once a year we would have a semiprogrammed meeting for worship with attention to the children.

In the early 1990s Marjean Liggett and I started a youth group made up of our Quaker teenagers and their friends. This group became a great success and source of the meeting's pride. We had a diverse, energetic group of teens who were always welcome at our monthly potluck suppers and special gatherings such as our annual retreat. The climax of this group was a trip we made to Washington, DC, in 1996. I wrote the following in my journal.

> In April one of my best friends, Larry Yates, the stepfather of my son's best friend, and I took seven high schoolers from our Quaker youth group to Washington to sit on the steps of the Lincoln Memorial and read Martin Luther King Jr.'s "I Have a Dream" speech. This was a mixed racial group, and I realized on the way up there why I had led this group to do this. This was the symbolic realization of that dream in our lives. For five years we had nurtured a youth group comprised of blacks and whites, boys and girls, protestant, Catholics, and Jews, into a cohesive, thoughtful group of friends. It was a community we were deeply proud of, for we were not only unique in composition, we had had some great experiences together.
>
> So on April 13, 1996, all nine of us, including black boys and white girls, white boys and black girls, and two men, one white, one black, read three paragraphs each of that inspired speech while a group of passing tourists and sojourners stopped to listen. For me that Saturday morning was the real Easter of 1996. Twenty-eight years before Dr. King had planted a seed in me to seek to live a life of inclusiveness and justice that this group represented. In our own little way our lives have become one of the many blooms from that initial seed.

There were other events in our meeting's life together of similar emotional and spiritual significance. Two stand out: the weddings we presided over, and clearness committees.

It is amazing to me what wisdom common people have to say about marriage and death. Growing up United Methodist I did not know this, for at weddings, funerals, and baptisms only the preacher spoke, normally. But at Quaker weddings and funerals, being unprogrammed, common people share wisdom that is just right for the persons and families involved. I have never been to a Quaker wedding or funeral where there were not three outstanding events. First, the worship would begin with tremendous anxiety (Is anyone going to speak? Will there be articulate words of comfort or advice?). Second, a surprising—no, awesome—expression of wisdom or comfort would come from an unpredictable speaker. Third, a genuine sense of awe would be expressed after the service at how deeply moving it was. If there is one thing Quakers do right, it is weddings and funerals. In taking the ordained clergy out of the primary role and giving it to those who know the celebrants or the grieving best, the wisdom expressed is incredible!

Our meeting found early on that we had a very special calling when people were embarking on married life together or gathering to grieve. We grew to trust the process of waiting on the Spirit so well that it was a source of great pride that we were lifting up a place where folks could express their deepest thoughts, feelings, and convictions. After every wedding we presided over, a dozen or so of us would stand around, shaking our heads in amazement at how profoundly touching the messages were, *and* at how unpredictable they had been! In addition, countless non-Quakers would exclaim how touched they were by the experience.

The other understanding that was growing on us was of what a clearness committee could do. Probably the most articulate expression of what a clearness committee is comes from Parker Palmer (1998). He writes, "A 'clearness committee' [is] a process in which the group refrains from giving you advice but spends three hours asking you honest, open questions to help you discover your own inner truth" (p. 152). The process begins when "the so-called focus person" invites four or five colleagues to be members of the committee. The focus person then writes "a few pages about the problem" for the committee to read.

The committee meets for two to three uninterrupted hours. Seated in a circle with the focus person, committee members practice the discipline of giving undivided attention to that person and his or her question. For two or more hours, the focus person becomes the heart of this small version of the community of truth, the sacred subject, worthy of respect. Palmer (1998) writes:

> This means that committee members do not call attention to themselves by laughing uproariously when something funny happens or by rushing to comfort the focus person when he or she is feeling pain or by falsely uniting with his or her concern ("I know exactly how you feel."). Undivided attention means forgetting about yourself, and for just a couple of hours, acting as if you had no other purpose on earth than to care for this human being.
>
> The meeting begins with the focus person briefly restating the issue. Then members of the committee begin their work, guided and constrained by the basic and nonnegotiable ground rule of this proceeding: *members are forbidden to speak to the focus person in any way except to ask that person an honest, open question.* The pace of the questioning must be slow—this is a discernment process, not a thesis defense or cross-examination. . . . By allowing ample silence between a response and the next question, the group keeps the process respectful and gentle. . . . Over a two hour period, this cycle of question and response can have remarkable cumulative effect. As the focus person speaks his or her truth, the layers of interference between that person and the inner teacher are slowly stripped away, allowing the person to hear more clearly the guidance that comes from within.
>
> As the process unfolds, we are reminded of a simple truth: because we cannot get inside another person's soul, we cannot possibly know the answer to another person's problem. Indeed, we cannot even know exactly what the problem is. . . . Watching the focus person in this setting provides the most vivid evidence . . . that each of us has a teacher within—all we need are the conditions that allow us to listen, to speak, and to learn. . . . Fifteen minutes before the [meeting] ends, someone asks the focus person if he or she wants to continue with the questions-only rule or would be willing to accept some mirroring [reflecting what was

said or did that he or she might not be fully aware of] in addition to more questions.

The meeting is concluded with two reminders: that "the value of the process is not to be judged by whether the . . . problem has been 'solved.' [Rather, it] is about planting seeds." Second, what went on is confidential. (Palmer, 1998, pp. 152-155)

Early in our life together we read Parker's description of the clearness committee and tried to follow his suggestions. We could not. Not only did we not have the patience to sit for three hours, we also would digress from questioning to conversation. But who cared? What mattered most was that we cared enough to volunteer to sit for an hour or two and hear one another. The experiences were not about following a prescription for us, they were exercises in listening and loving one another. Inevitably, they were deeply moving, insightful experiences. It became not a symptom of desperation to ask for a clearness committee, but a signal that we wanted to be closer to one another. I still marvel at how easy it is for Friends in our meeting to ask for help. It is as if the clearness committee has become not a way to humble oneself to some counseling but a way to enjoy wrestling with life with others who also wrestle with life at its points of difficulty. Clearness committees in our meeting became almost as unpredictable as weddings and funerals! We *tried* to follow Parker's prescription, but we just could not follow the letter of the law. However, we found the spirit of the law! Even Parker would be pleased with how well we stayed true to the essence of the clearness committee, for we truly let the Spirit have its way.

And when the Spirit leads, *everyone* is transformed! As the old spiritual says, "You gotta sing when the Spirit says sing . . . You gotta clap when the Spirit says clap . . . You gotta pray when the Spirit says pray." When the Spirit says sing/clap/pray that's what you gotta do! Our meeting was learning how to let the Spirit have its way.

Naturally, we wanted to share our strengths. We wanted to grow some. We found better locations, committed ourselves to higher rent and more visibility, and developed organizational ways to invite people into our community.

In the mid-1990s we began to search for a meetinghouse to purchase, an effort that became a source of conflict that taught me something more about community. I was the leader of this effort, for I felt strongly that we were at a point in our lives together at which a meetinghouse would help us become a stronger presence in Memphis and enrich our lives together. I also was concerned that our youth group was in need of a home base that our rental property did not adequately provide, and without a meetinghouse the youth group might die.

Quaker process is built around developing consensus—a sense of unity. We call it discerning the "sense of meeting." One of the main reasons small numbers of Quakers have had great influence on our culture is because of this sense of unity. When people truly find unity on a position they enhance that position's power greatly. What we found in our meeting were a few who were passionate about buying a meetinghouse and a few who were strongly opposed to particular choices or the timing of the purchase. We simply could not reach unity, so we did not make any purchase. I was deeply disappointed.

I had a choice. I could nurse my disappointment, watch some of the weaknesses of our meeting get weaker from our inaction—which I was convinced was ahead—and essentially pull away from the community, or I could focus on other aspects of our community life that would give me continued meaning. I admit that I was disappointed to the point of anger about our inaction, so part of me was quite reluctant to refocus my attention, and I didn't for a while. I just stewed, quietly and passively. One day, though, something occurred that drew me away from nursing my anger.

A young couple, Shiloh and Steven, came to our meeting looking for a place to be married. As we got to know them there reemerged a strong sense of what Quakerism is about—not just what *we* were about. There's a difference. As a Quaker meeting we carried the torch of Quaker principles, but our daily concerns often took precedence over foundational beliefs. Quakerism is about a simple, honest, and peaceful approach to life in which we meet normal anxieties and sadness with quietness and openness. Perhaps this is our transcendent vision. Our Quaker meeting—and particularly me—often becomes mired in discussion, conflicting desires, and disappointments. We had lost some of our quietness, but this new couple was not nearly as interested in our creature concerns as they were our commitment to simplicity and peacefulness. They were drawn to our quietness. In their fascination, they drew us back to our central foundation.

Shiloh and Steven had never attended a Quaker meeting before, but they saw something in us that I, in my disappointment, had lost sight of. Unlike me, they were not seeking to create growth or a meetinghouse to express our coming of age. They weren't wanting us to become more important—or as I expressed it, "a light to the city." They simply were open to us, open with us, and hoping to find us open to them. In short, they came to us in faith—for faith means openness.

Jean Vanier (1979), founder of L'Arche community for the mentally handicapped and their helpers in France, wrote in *Community and Growth* about a different kind of growth than that which I have been writing. I have been suggesting that our American view of growth is numerical and, past a certain point (or number), numerical growth—whether it be numbers of members, of programs, or of money—is a detriment to community. Vanier suggests that communities need a different kind of growth: growth in love and wisdom. (James Hillman (1996) calls this our need to grow downward.) "The more a community grows and puts down roots, the more it must discover its own deep meaning and own philosophy of life." Community, implies Vanier, consists of people in authentic relationships, not just "a gathering of 'doers',"but people seeking answer's to life's deepest questions (suffering, death, healing, wholeness, roles, sexuality, family). Thus a community connects with all of humanity and must bear fruit and reach out (Vanier, 1979, p. 117).

Vanier suggests that what happened to me is common among those in community, for growth in community is slow. After all the work I had put in trying to lead our meeting to the purchase of a meetinghouse, I felt let down, disappointed, and alone. "Members of a community have to be friends of time" (Vanier, 1979, pp. 124-125). I was not a friend of time.

Shiloh and Stephen drew me back to the real vision and spirit of our meeting, helping me to be recaptured by "the vision and spirit of the community" (Vanier, 1979, p. 131). I personally may have needed the humility of "failure" and disappointment in order to rediscover our fundamental vision. Vanier says that community becomes more open because it becomes more humble (Vanier, 1979). Our meeting was founded on a common vision of simplicity, honesty, and peace, supported by the weekly experience of mostly silent, unprogrammed worship. That vision did not need an owned meetinghouse.

As our vision expands, an owned meetinghouse might be called for, but my problem was that my sense of timing was hurried. Vanier describes such community tensions as similar to the pains of childbirth:

"The pain keeps each one little and humble; it keeps them calling out to God in prayer; it keeps them also struggling to understand and to love truth over and above their own ideas" (Vanier, 1979, p. 124).

What was difficult for me was waiting for that new reality or new vision. As important as our meeting's original vision was, it seemed to me that we had grown to a place where that vision was not open and visible enough for the larger community around us. I was asking a new question: how could we witness to our beliefs and work for peace and justice in the world? The wisdom of the community was that we were not ready for an owned meetinghouse, which I, in my egotism, had trouble accepting. We had to find another way.

Vanier (1979) distinguishes between a community's vision and its mission.

> The mission of a community is to give life to others, that is to say, to transmit new hope and new meaning to them. Mission is revealing to others their fundamental beauty, value and importance to the universe, their capacity to love, to grow and to do beautiful things and to meet God. (p. 86)

Part of what Shiloh and Stephen found was that mission. Within our meeting, their gifts were being affirmed; they were finding that we were lifting up their capacity to love and be spiritual beings. This was happening without an owned meetinghouse! But, Vanier (1979) warns, "when communities become rich, self-satisfied, proud of their competence and power . . . they can no longer be instruments of the life of God. *They give what they have, which is their self-satisfaction* (pp. 87-88, emphasis mine). I now suspect that the wisdom of our meeting community was that were we to purchase a meetinghouse when *I* wanted it we might have become "rich, self-satisfied, and proud." Then we could have joined the many churches in Memphis that grow big and powerful at the expense of true community—community that includes poverty and humility.

Many times in my life I have found myself enamored with my own gifts and potential. Inevitably two things happen during those periods. First, I work hard to hone that potential and am able to enhance my talent and abilities. Second, I bite off more than I can chew. For me personally this dynamic develops concerning some career move. I will find myself becoming good enough at a certain skill that I begin getting recognition for it. That recognition spurs my imagination:

what if I had a more powerful position and better pay for the expression of this skill? I begin to look for something more for myself, and I usually find a golden opportunity of some sort. Seizing the opportunity, I find myself swept along in a river of change and excitement. Then, out of the blue, an event occurs that brings me back to shore, regrounds me. This event is almost always humbling experience—an accurate criticism, a glaring mistake, an unexpected rejection, a poor evaluation. At first I am usually outraged and defensive, but after I gain some objective distance from my emotional reaction, I gain the insight that I am a man of many shortcomings who needs to seek forgiveness at every turn. Giving out of self-satisfaction is disabling in the long run.

Communities are similar to this. When they become self-satisfied they ignore their shortcomings. The inevitable tensions become "a call to a new fidelity" (Vanier, 1979, p. 121). I believe that one of the purposes of community is to encourage dialogue, reflection, and personal growth. In other words, communities create philosophers. It does this by diminishing our natural fear of conflict. Deep down we are all afraid of conflict, for it often leads to split ups, abandonment, and even betrayal. M. Scott Peck (1988) suggests that this leads to what he calls "pseudocommunity"—polite, superficial interactions that avoid conflict, differences, and the truth. Peck says that true community happens after a pseudocommunity begins to wrestle with its inherent conflicts—emptying itself of the illusion of peace. Paradoxically, this emptying lifts up conflict while also creating the peace within the community members. The peace of community is born out of labor and pain. Or, we might say, resurrection does not occur without a prior cross.

Vanier (1979) says that the mission of a community is to be "a sign of a suffering Church. But a community which prays and loves is a sign of resurrection" (p. 85). Peck (1988) uses the word *emptying* where Vanier uses *prays*. I'd suggest that the emptying prayers of the community are its encounter with conflict and struggle. Out of that suffering comes new life—the life of community.

In the 1990s, our meeting wrestled with a mission statement:

The Memphis Friends Meeting's mission is to do the following:

• provide an alternative worship experience that is relevant to our daily lives

- be a sanctuary for the acceptance of differences
- live together in the Light of the testimonies of Peace, Equality, Simplicity, and Integrity

Although we never sought unity with this, the words shed some light on what I felt drawn back to when Shiloh and Steven came to our Meeting. Not everything about community mission is dependent on money. Buying a meetinghouse is dependent on money, but community is not. Vanier (1979) writes a poignant statement that addresses this:

> Communities and their members are called to be poor and do impossible things, such as build community and bring healing, reconciliation, forgiveness and wholeness to people. Mission is to bring the life of God to others, and *this can only be done if community and people are poor and humble,* letting the love of God flow through them.
>
> Mission implies this double poverty, but also trust in the call and the power of God manifested through poverty, littleness and humility.
>
> In the degree that people and communities are rich, self-satisfied, proud of their competence and power, and want to do things that they know they are capable of doing, then they can no longer be instruments of the life of God. They give what they have, which is their self-satisfaction. (pp. 87-88)

In some ways this is the most radical statement I know about community—especially for an American. In the United States we are used to testing the vitality of community by its growth and wealth. The Church Health Center is a perfect example. During the first ten years of the Church Health Center's existence we raised 5 percent more money than we spent, always giving us the freedom to expand and grow. Yet that growing wealth was also the major factor in growing beyond the capacity of the original community and the subsequent rise of an institutional ministry.

I have a friend, Billy Vaughan, who is the dean of the Memphis School of Servant Leadership, a dynamic and life-changing but financially struggling faith formation school. Billy has often told me of his ambivalence about financial security for the school. The school was set up to function as a community and to serve the poor and downtrodden. If the school were to become wealthy, Billy argued, it would lose its sense of faith, for its faith was founded on risk. Students and faculty at the school found their identification with the oppressed partly in the insecurity of the school, which was reflected in its finances. If the school were not poor, how could it understand poverty? If the school did not wrestle with finances, how could it show our culture a way to transcend financial insecurities (the fear of not having enough)? By living with scarcity, the school community had to find a sense of inner abundance.

Of course, I was part of the Church Health Center when it was growing in scope of ministry and wealth. Clearly, part of its growth was our clarity of mission; part was the ability of our executive director to raise funds. What I was most fascinated with was how central a mission statement was, and that staying true to that mission kept an organization on track, focused, and capable of being highly magnetic. I took that interest to our meeting, leading most of our discussions about our mission. What I wanted to do was to help us grow, but now that I look back at it, I believe if the meeting were to have followed my leadership we might have grown beyond our capacity to be a community.

This raises a central question of the vital community: what are the limits of community in relation to growth and size? Very large churches inevitably create communities within the church. Sunday school classes are designed to function as communities, programs are created to give small groups of people community experiences, and various committees of the church are communities. As I stated earlier, the most common statement I have heard from members of megachurches is "It's large, but it feels small." This occurs because of the subcultures that can develop into communities. So large organizations can, in fact, spawn communities. Organized well, they do well.

I think that the key, though, is not how organized a large corporation or church is, it is the depth of commitment to those who are different and suffering. Megachurches are also notorious for fostering a homogeneous congregation. They are not filled with true diversity—not racially, not culturally, and not politically or philosophically.

Our meeting has, in my opinion, been revitalized by the infusion of people such as Shiloh and Steven, for they have reminded us of what is more fundamental than growth—it is quiet peacefulness that leads to caring for one another and those who suffer. We still are small enough to know one another personally. We still have a deep commitment to children. We still effectively use unprogrammed worship and clearness committees. We still care deeply for the larger world around us.

Our meeting has stayed together as a community for nearly twenty years now. We've lost some key members in our daily life together, but when they return to visit, we catch up quickly and are excited about introducing our new Friends to the old ones. We've continued to nurture ourselves inwardly, and we continue to encourage and support one another in our activist efforts in the larger world. Occasionally we find ourselves drawn together to do work that is meant to relieve suffering—peace work, ecological work, work for justice—but mostly we send one another out to do good work as individuals. Often we wish we could find a common activity that would sustain us for some time, but those activities have tended to be short-lived. Our community, however, has survived. I believe it has mainly because we have not been split apart by power struggles, whether over purchasing a meetinghouse or some other issue. We've had power struggles and personality conflicts, but we've been fortunate enough to let them go. Why? I think it's because we've felt the vitality of our community and know that it is worth more than a political victory.

As proud as we are of our community, it may just be that humility has saved us. I know it saved me, for when I "lost" the meetinghouse initiative I found a sort of salvation in the humility the loss gave me. I credit this mainly to no one gloating in my humility—which would have turned it into humiliation and probably have made me very angry. Instead, we sat quietly, sought peace, and learned to love again.

We remain small, but like those touched by the Church Health Center's early community, one cannot help but notice the strength of leadership our members bring into various civic and professional organizations throughout the city, state, and nation.

Over and over again I notice that communities create people who achieve at a higher level then would otherwise be expected. I have no doubt that a key factor in a community's nurturance of its members is that it chooses depth over breadth, strength over power, and this is usually represented as a limit in its size. What makes this choice particularly hard is that we live in a culture that defines success in size and numbers. But they are false measures for community. Size and numbers may measure the success of an organization or political activity, but communities have a different standard to live up to: quality of relationships.

Many of the members of our meeting have become leaders in the Southeast regional gathering of Quakers called the Southern Appalachian Yearly Meeting and Association of the Religious Society of Friends (SAYMA).

Once when I was the coordinator for the children's program of SAYMA I hired a leader of the Catholic Catechesis of the Good Shepherd movement, Rebekah Rojcewicz, to teach us some of the principles of this highly successful method of religious instruction for children.

Rebekah organized the children into two groups: three- to six-year-olds and seven- to eleven-year-olds. Within the older group we had a few very interested children and a few children who bordered on cynicism. Quakers kids are often that way, for the shadow side of the independence and freedom of expression with which Quaker kids are often raised is a tendency to think that only their ideas are good, that adults do not have fun or good ideas, and the kids become cynical. The oldest and biggest boys in the group were such cynical leaders, which caused us many problems. They resisted our leadership. In addition, two of them were brothers who fought one another constantly. It became a very difficult group to work with.

On the morning of our third day together we were hopeful that we had made some progress towards reeling these older kids in—that maybe they were ready to join in on some of what we had to offer them. We gathered peacefully to music and soft conversation. A number of adult volunteers gathered around as well, which we felt would help contain the previous conflict. Some of those volunteers were there in part because they were curious about Rebekah's approach to religious education for children. Some were, in fact, national leaders within the Society of Friends.

Just before we started our activities, the two brothers began to fight. I calmly and peacefully went to them, thinking that laying hands on them they would calm down and stop. They didn't. In fact, they fought harder. I lay my hands on them harder—that is, I started trying to pull them apart. They fought harder. Frustrated, I yanked them apart, and they started kicking each other, so I angrily shoved one of the boys across the room. I guess they decided that my show of force was worse than continuing to fight each other, so they stopped. Then I saw that the older brother had his brother's name tag, which was the reason for the fight. I told him to give me the name tag, and when he did not I angrily ripped it from his hand.

The fight was over, the boys were separated and staying put, but I wanted to crawl in a hole and hide my embarrassment before these peace-loving Quaker leaders. I figured they must have been thinking, "So *this* is Quaker religious education at SAYMA." Rebekah tried to draw the children into a song, but they all sat there looking at me, standing there flustered, embarrassed, and paralyzed. I think I squeaked out, "I wish that hadn't happened."

The man next to me, the father of one of our children, put his hand on me as if to say, "That's all right," and I sat down and let Rebekah pull the group back together and shift the attention from the conflict.

Most of the rest of the day went okay, until that evening when a visitor brought with her a very enjoyable program to share with the children. When it came time to interact with her, though, our older boys resisted again until one of our volunteers went over to try to coax them in. The oldest boy—one of the brothers—would not budge, so the volunteer pulled on him forcibly. I went over to help, and seeing that they were getting into a very familiar power struggle that could not be won, I said, "I'm not going to force you to participate, but I am very disappointed." We left him alone and went back to the program leader. He ran off and sat down on the driveway above where we were.

After the program ended, four of his friends went to where he was and returned to me to tell me he was crying. I went to him and found him slumped over, head in his hands, sobbing quietly. I asked what was wrong, but he would not answer. The children asked me why he was crying, and I said, "I think I hurt his feelings when I told him I was disappointed." He nodded yes, then blurted out, "I'm a terrible person! I'm just a bad boy!" Then he slumped back down and covered his face.

Immediately, all four children with him said, "No, you're not!"

He popped up again and shouted, "Yes, I am. I've been in a psychiatric hospital two times. That's where they put bad boys. I'm terrible!"

The children asked, "What's a psychiatric hospital?"

He did not answer, and I said, "It's not a place where they put bad people. It's a place where people go who need help, and we all need help."

I turned to the children and asked them, "Why do you think he's not a bad person?"

Two of them said to him, "Because you're nice to me." One boy, whose father had touched me in the morning after my eruption, reached out, touched him, and said, "Because you are my friend." The smallest boy said, "Because you're nice to me most of the time."

Soon the cloud lifted, and we sat on the ground and talked about our experiences together for about twenty minutes, then went away for the night.

I thought for days about that boy telling his friend he wasn't bad because "you are my friend." To me it was the best of what Quakerism is truly about. Our formal name is the Society of Friends, and I think that little boy's touch captured why.

We are not good people because we are good. We are good because we are befriended. Being a friend makes us good. We are not good because we avoid being bad or going to psychiatric hospitals. We are good because we are friends—because we are loved. Perhaps that is the true standard of measurement for community: that we can be friends.

Chapter 8

The Revolving Nature
of Communities

Early Christianity was built on community life. It began with the community of the early disciples, gained momentum with the magnetic experience at Pentecost, developed identity with Paul's missionary work, and became cohesive through its early theological thought, captured in the New Testament. It is helpful to understand the development of community in early Christian life.

To see early Christianity as only about following Christ is not the full story. Such an assertion is actually impossible, for Christ was a name Paul popularized, adding it to Jesus. Were it not for Paul, Jesus would have been known as Jesus, not Jesus Christ. Early Christianity was, in fact, a Jesus movement. It became the Christian religion when it became institutionalized. But even then, Christianity was a religion that had abundant room for some very divergent perspectives.

Looking at the early Christian community sheds light on what it means to be a community. The essence of what makes any religion great is its contribution to true community. It is in community that people are changed, that peace is accomplished, that justice is lifted up. More than anything else, communities give movements life. Yet maintaining community life is a struggle that revolves from life to death. Understanding the revolving nature of community life can help us create true communities. Studying early Christianity is a study of community life.

Four healthy, life-giving branches of Christianity exist, as well as a branch of legalism that, unfortunately, might be the most dominant, and is alienating and destructive. Every Christian denomination has elements of all five branches, and seeing ourselves as part of a stream of history can help us reform ourselves to the better.

doi:10.1300/5653_09

JUDAISM AT THE TIME OF JESUS

Judaism during the time of Jesus was not a particularly attractive religion in the Roman Empire. Early Greek thinking that so deeply influenced the Western world was dualistic in its orientation, separating mind and body and lifting up philosophical thought and human actualization. Israelites paid more attention to stories and rules than to thought, and as a result Judaism was more monistic than dualistic—it lifted up oneness, not separating human life into two elements. Judaism was also monotheistic in a culture that that was multitheistic. Israelite Rabbis, furthermore, were very serious about their religion. It wasn't very magnetic, but chose instead to hang onto its own.

At its best Judaism was about remembering the Torah story—that Yahweh delivered the Israelites out of the house of bondage to the promised land—in a way that gave them a sense of God's love for them as a people. As a result of this relationship, Israelites found a "happy obedience"—what we might today call the disciplined life. The Torah was, they understood, not just a story—it was a way of life. Hence, Torah was both myth and law. The myth gave them an identity and community. The law helped them delight in being good. Sin was seen as deviation from the law or Torah.

At its worst, Judaism was restrictive, exclusive, and legalistic. During Jesus' day the Pharisees were deeply concerned with the erosion of Judaism to Roman and other world influences. They felt Judaism needed reform. Their method was to call for greater discipline—to lift up law—and ask Israelites to close their ranks again and live a life more pleasing to God. They also taught about a new life—the resurrection of the dead into a new life. They would assert that though you might not feel the happiness of living a good life now, a new life is ahead for good people after they die, so be good for future rewards.

Jesus was actually a fan of the Pharisaic reform movement. He once said that the Pharisees sit on the seat of Moses (Matthew 23:2), for he knew that they were right about the need for reform. Judaism was becoming both a religion for the comfortable—a feel-good religion—and a legalistic religion that was quite judgmental and aggressive toward those who did not adhere to the law. It was not a religion that truly helped people live a just and generous life, pleasing to God and helping to create community. Similar to the Pharisees, Jesus was a reformer, but he saw the Pharisees leaning towards legalism and exclusivism. Jesus' teachings were a protest against both nonsacrificial religion and legalism, a call to altruism to all, and an assertion that the kingdom of God was at hand—not a place to get to after death.

Charles Shelton's (1935) *In His Steps* vision is an example of this kind of religious community. Shelton's vision was of community that would imitate Christ. Throughout his book he described community life to be similar to what Jesus was creating: gatherings of believers who shared in common and deeply emotional commitments to others. In his imaginary community were constant reminders of the transforming power of the members' decision to imitate Christ, how it radically changed their lives and made them supremely happy and brazenly courageous. At each gathering they would remind one another of the stories of change and how much happier they felt in following "in His steps." Their obedience to their promise was a happy obedience—an excellent example of a movement similar to the best of Judaism that Jesus was positive about.

Unfortunately, that very same liberation Shelton's characters found is often swallowed up in insecurities and fears that make people rigid, legalistic, and exclusive. The "WWJD" bracelets and emblems so often worn now are sometimes more a sign to others that the wearers are part of an elite group—the "saved"—that sets them apart and judges those who might believe differently. In fact, Shelton's approach did not include a statement of faith, but was a decision to act. It was an ethical vow that led to a radical sharing with those less fortunate, not a sign or set of beliefs that set them apart.

Jesus himself was raised and nurtured in such an atmosphere. Within the Israelite society were both radical thinkers just as intent upon reform as Shelton's characters as well as exclusivists who would have Jews snub any who were not in accord with their rigid beliefs.

INCLUSIVE VERSUS EXCLUSIVE COMMUNITIES

No community exists that is not exclusive. In community life, standards of behavior include some that simply cannot be crossed. If a person comes into a community, finds an openness and acceptance, then announces, for example, that he or she is an active pedophile and thinks being a pedophile is appropriate, the community might dialogue with him or her over the orientation, but will—I would hope—

eventually exclude the person and banish him or her from the community (and then call the cops). An more moderate example would be a community that does not accept someone who espouses an unacceptable belief. For example, if a Christian who believes that Jews are going to hell were to try to join a synagogue in order to convert Jews, it would be appropriate for that community to exclude that Christian. Now if the Christian joined without trying to convert Jews to Christianity but simply had different beliefs that he or she did not try to push onto others, no grounds for dismissal would exist. An inclusive community can tolerate differences.

The real problem with exclusivism is when it goes beyond behavior to attributes. When people are excluded for their skin color, sex, sexual orientation, economic class, or background—in other words, when people are excluded because of who they are, not because of what they do—this is a kind of exclusivism that is a deterrent to community. Why? Because it makes a group protective and legalistic. If rights and privileges are denied because of attributes instead of behavior, time is wasted defending attributes instead of helping community members become whole and healthy.

Inclusive communities are not based on prejudice. Although they do have standards that allow that some can and should be excluded, those standards are based upon behavior, not attributes that they are prejudiced against.

I have experienced inappropriate exclusivism in more groups than not. It is prevalent in liberal and conservative political groups. I've seen liberal groups deeply prejudiced against Republicans, and conservative groups that loathe liberals. I've seen African-American groups prejudiced against whites, and God knows plenty of whites groups are notoriously racist. Inappropriate exclusivism is not confined to any one sector of society.

The key factor in inappropriate exclusivism is power. When people in a group do not feel they possess enough power, they worry about their boundaries, their ability to uphold their standards, and their cohesiveness. Not feeling powerful enough, they assert their power in inappropriate ways—a kind of pseudopower. They exclude those whom they feel threatened by. In contrast, when people in a group feel internally confident, they possess power that is self-contained. Such groups are not easily threatened by differences. They can let different people in. They can entertain the possibility of change—even if it challenges their standards. This does not mean they will abandon their principles, it means that they are not legalistic about them. Legalism is about codifying power, and groups that are confident in their self-contained power don't need legalism. Legalism is evidence of a lack of confidence, and groups that are legalistic tend to be inappropriately exclusive. They are trying to hang on to power that they have not yet found. The easy—but wrong—way to do so is to find a scapegoat or a person or group of people to exclude based on prejudice. Inclusive groups do not need such pseudopower. They find their power from within—a type of spiritual power.

THE ETHICAL MYSTICISM OF JESUS

Such spiritual power was central to Jesus' experience and message. The defining experience in Jesus' early ministry was his mystical experience in the desert. Without that experience, his ministry would have been just another behavioral reform. With it, Jesus presented what can be called "ethical mysticism." Because of his mysticism, Jesus saw the *spirit* of the law. Sin, for Jesus, was deviation from the spirit of the law. Jesus taught that life lived in a manner pleasing to God—who was an Abba, a warm daddy—was both celebratory and sacrificial. Because it was new life, the kingdom of God "at hand," people could go ahead and party! Jesus was greatly appreciated and roundly criticized for his party habits. He had fun on the Sabbath, changed water into wine, ate much, hung around the wilder and less disciplined elements of society—probably even did a great amount of laughing! When the disciples were sent out to find out what people said about Jesus, they came back with the word that people thought he might be another John the Baptist, Elijah, or one of the prophets—the biblical wildmen. They didn't report that Jesus was meek and mild, did they? Jesus was serious about life beginning on earth—for him it was not just existence, but Life! It included, and centered around, love—a love so special, so strong, that it was sacrificial. Jesus, as much as any teacher who has ever lived, showed us how love wraps itself around us in a warmly sensual and happy way. He also taught us an incredible willingness to be sacrificial—even to death. Part of how he taught this was because he, similar to the Pharisees, was sure that death did not end life—the kingdom of God is from now on.

Often we see parallels to this kind of community in which people dance or play together. Later in this book I will introduce you to a dance community in which participants share in a celebration of life, sexuality, and movement that makes them care little about fatigue, worries, and differences for their two or three hours of dancing. It is this kind of celebratory community that Jesus lifted up, helping people to feel the realization of the kingdom of God. Accompanying this celebratory community is a love that makes people willing to give themselves to others. When a dancer in a community such as the one I will refer to takes ill or gets injured, an enormous outpouring of caring occurs—the kind of sacrificial love or compassion that Jesus also embodied and encouraged.

The longer I live the more convinced I am that the greatest gift we have for one another is sacrificial love. I don't mean the kind of sacrifice that women have traditionally *had* to make for men to blossom—the kind that is really about oppression and sexism—but the kind that is chosen so that another might live. It's the kind that is expressed in the story of a four-year-old boy who, when asked if he might give a pint of blood for his year-old sister, hesitated a moment before consenting, and as his blood was being drawn asked, "When do I die?" That is the kind of sacrificial love that Jesus was lifting up.

MYSTICAL UNION AND PAUL

Jesus, by himself, did not create Christianity. In fact, if Paul and John had not come along, Christianity would never have become a world religion. It would have been a small Jesus movement. Why? Because Jesus' views were more Jewish than Greek. Judaism was destined to remain a smaller movement because of its focus on a particular story and a strict lifestyle. Although Jesus tried to reform Judaism, he himself did not fully break from Judaism's inwardness. It was Paul who really created Christianity.

Paul, when he was called Saul before his conversion, was similar to Jesus: an advocate of Pharisaic reform. Unlike Jesus, however, he believed that reform needed to be in the discipline of the law, not in interpreting the spirit of the law. Furthermore, he was upset with the early disciples' claim that Jesus was resurrected from the dead. Pharisees thought that resurrection occurred, just not on earth. Saul thought the disciples of Jesus were perverting Judaism, so he participated in their persecution. After helping to stone and kill Stephen, Saul, traveling to Damascus, was struck blind by a mystical experience that changed him. Jesus had been touched with light and had visions in the desert; Paul was struck with light and blinded—but the results were similar. Jesus went soon afterward into his ministry to the Jews. Paul went soon afterward into his ministry into the Greco-Roman world, helping Roman citizens to see this Jesus movement in a way that included them. Paul made Christianity attractive to the rest of the world.

How did he do this? He did it in three ways: (1) creating a theology that answered questions first posed by ancient Greek philosophers, (2) offering a more moderate political perspective on the Jesus movement—more transforming but less politically revolutionary, and (3) teaching a morality based on love and community, not on obedience and legalism.

In contrast to early Judaism, Paul was deeply influenced by Platonic dualism—the view that body and mind are separate, and mind is superior. I heard writer Alan Watts assert in a lecture in the 1970s that Paul created the most sexually hung up religion ever, but Paul's purpose in lifting up the spirit and de-emphasizing the "flesh" was more about answering the Greco-Roman idea of dualism than messing with sex and sexuality. People in the Roman world resonated with his way of thinking. He also used a line of logical argument that followed Greek ideals. His explanation of the contrast between law and grace was very logical and reasonable—it made sense to the people who had been raised under the influence of the Greek philosophers.

The fundamental starting point of Paul's theology was in combining a Greek idea—the Christ—with Jesus. It was Paul who put Christ and Jesus together, expanding the idea of a Jesus movement—a movement following Jesus' teachings—to a movement that was more than, different than, Judaism. In fact, with Paul, the teachings of Jesus were not particularly important, at least not more so than the teachings of the ancient Greek philosophers. It was the union of Christ and Jesus that was truly important to Paul, for in that union—that Jesus was adopted by or sent by God and therefore became the Christ—humankind was forever redeemed.

In his letter to the Romans Paul articulates his most logical theological argument. He writes that "the righteousness of God has been manifested apart from the law . . . through faith in Jesus Christ for all who believe . . . for all have sinned and fall short of the glory of God, and are justified by [God's] grace as a gift, through the redemption that is in Christ Jesus" (Romans 3:21-24, English Standard Version). In passages such as this, Paul asserts that a mystical union is available for all that overcomes the divided will, which is sin. Paul teaches that an inner change is available through grace that comes through faith in Christ Jesus. This life of faith means that law no longer dominates our lives. Of course, this is the teaching of a man who had been obsessed with law. He had been a fanatical reformer of the law, one who would hold Stephen's cloak while Stephen was being stoned to death. Paul, then known as Saul, was not a happily obedient Jew. He himself was tormented by the law. Thus, when he had a mystical experience on the road to Damascus that gave him a new perspective on the life of faith—a life that freed one from being enslaved by law—he was overwhelmed with freedom and love. He wrote, "For freedom Christ has set us free" (Galatians 5:1, ESV).

Paul lifted up faith and belief to new heights of human nobleness. Belief has the character of *active hope*. When we actively hope, we allow ourselves to be emptied and open to the brink of despair. Paul writes, "Who will deliver me from this body of death?" (Romans 7:24, ESV). We are totally undefended, hoping against data and reason for something to help us take the next step. Paul has found it! Faith is the free gift God gives us when we hope for that which seems beyond hope—an end to this life of pain and weakness. Through our faith, our deep, trusting openness, God's grace accepts us even in our sinfulness and pain. For Paul, the openness of faith becomes a channel through which you and I are reunited with God. Faith is therefore a way of peace, a reconciling posture. Faith offers a new ethic that calls a person to be less defensive, less defended, and more open and accepting of others and differences. Faith, in Paul's thinking, is beyond reason—it is unbelievable!

Faith, for Paul, is the key to his theology. It is different than belief. Belief stops short. It puts our hopes into a box to affirm or deny. Faith takes our hopes out of the box and gives us a sense of openness. The life of faith is one in which we deeply and profoundly experience all of what life has to offer, which opens us up to both suffering and joy—and most importantly to God's free gift of grace, the experience of the sublime, beautiful, and holy.

Thus, Paul's mystical experience and theology has inspired mystics throughout history. This inspiration is not confined to famous mystics. It is available to everyone. Dorothee Soelle (2001), in her book *The Silent Cry: Mysticism and Resistance,* makes a convincing case that mysticism is a common experience, found in the eye-opening experiences of compassion, sensuality, community, and beauty. When we see something and exclaim, "Wow!"—that's a mystical experience. It might not be a revelation on the road to Damascus, but it is a mystical moment. Strung together, such moments are part of what makes the life of faith so dramatically different than life without faith.

The shadow side of Paul was that he was so intent on building the Church that he often expressed prejudicial views that have been used to oppress people for centuries. Though meant to help the community function more efficiently, Paul's words have been used to justify sexism, racism, homophobia, and even prejudice against long hair. Although Paul would not have used his own injunctions to give people reason to exclude others inappropriately, his injuctions have nonetheless been used to do so. Still, Paul's main concern was reconciliation, community, and the life of faith, which no amount of perversion of his time-bound injunctions can erase.

We see this theology expressed in communities in which openness and sharing is encouraged. Groups that begin sharing a simple task together, such as studying a particular subject, doing a manual job, organizing for a specific task, or governing an organization, often find in the middle of their mutuality, community. A sudden expression of vulnerability from one of their members is met with openness and vulnerability from others in the group, shifting it from group to community. The groups I have been in that make this transition are unforgettable experiences. They have a gracefulness about them that is liberating. It is what Paul taught, encouraged, and led people to.

John's Communion with the Loving God

The apostle John gives us an even clearer way to create community. Whereas Paul gave us a way to help individuals find a new and healthier way of life, John gives the Church a way to celebrate one another. His writings lift up community.

How? By lifting up the idea of God as a loving father who would sacrifice his only son so that we might live. John teaches about a God whose love was unimaginable, and by living fully in the love of God we will love one another in ways that make community possible.

Unfortunately, John's Gospel is loaded with sayings that are used by some Christians in alienating ways. Christians far too often use John's phrases to condemn anyone who does not believe just what they do. It is sickening how the fundamental message of John—that God is more interested in people accepting one another, seeking reconciliation, and experiencing the love of God that makes us love one another—gets replaced with a legalistic orthodoxy that separates and condemns. It's bad enough that the writings of Paul are used as justification for condemning people who are different or prefer liberation to subservience. But with John's writings, some Christians take the condemnation up another notch and attack those who simply *think* differently. They miss the point.

John's good news is that "For God so loved the world that he gave his only son, that whoever believes in Him should not perish but have eternal life" (John 3:16, ESV). The emphasis is on God's love, *not* on the necessity for the correct belief! Paul Tillich (1948) interpreted such a call for belief as "accepting acceptance." In other words, in spite of our shortcomings we are accepted, and all we have to do is accept that acceptance and our lives will be changed from mere existence to real Life, from now on, everlasting life.

In what might be the most beloved story in the Bible, a story that is often placed in the center of John's account of Jesus' life, some men bring a sinful woman to Jesus for him to judge her fate, which would legally be stoning. Jesus replies, "Let him who is without sin among you be the first to throw a stone at her" (John 8:7, ESV). All leave, and Jesus refuses to condemn her as well. He tells her, "Go, and from now on sin no more" (John 8:11, ESV).

I imagine she went away relieved, probably deeply transformed, but still sinned some more. For that's the way people are, even those who are transformed by God's grace. We still sin and fall short of the will of God. But that is not the point of the story. The love of God, expressed in the person of Jesus, was what the story is about. It is a love that even the worst sin could not destroy. The woman didn't even ask for acquittal, either. It was a free gift.

In Victor Hugo's (1862) story *Les Miserables* the thief Jean Valjean is caught with a bishop's silver. The bishop, though, instead of fingering Jean Valjean, tells the police that the silver was a gift for Jean, and offers him his silver candlesticks as well. Later he tells Valjean that he does not care much for riches, and that the silver might very well change Valjean's life because the bishop had purchased the thief's soul. He told Valjean that he no longer belonged to the devil, but to God. This too was the message of John.

John begins with two universal images: the Logos and the Light, which are unifying principles: "If we walk in the Light . . . we have fellowship with one another" (I John 1:7, ESV). Howard Brinton (1967) suggests that For John the word of God (Logos) is a source of unity between God and humankind (this idea of the Logos is borrowed from the Jewish philosopher Philo, who saw the Logos as a dynamic unifying source) or "the agency by which the creative Yahweh [the Lord] operates" and is revealed to the world (Jones, 1952, p. 53). The Logos not only redeems one from personal inadequacy but also joins people in true communion with one another and with God. In addition, John offers an alternative to Paul's dualism of flesh and spirit. For John the Word became flesh. John offers a union of body and soul that allows sensuality an acceptable place in one's life. John viewed God as a benevolent father who smiles on his people, and his people are all people who are saved by the life and light of Christ. Quakers use the expressions *reached* or *tendered* to help interpret this gentle persuasion from a loving father God that John wrote of. Christ, for John, was "a living presence felt by mystical intuition" (Brinton, 1967, p. 29) that brought people together.

The Hendrix track team I wrote about in Chapter 3 is a good example of such a Johannine community. As we became skilled at the art and science of running fast we began to realize how our spirit and our bodies were one and how our team support could make us all do better. The spirit of the team was connected to our physical performances. Furthermore, we were blessed with a loving coach whom we not only respected and learned from, we loved. He taught us more about life than about running. We learned from him how to live, and living right meant, for us, doing our best and doing it in support of and with the support of our teammates. Winning was not as important as doing our best and lifting us all up to higher standards of life. This was the kind of community of love that John presented.

ORTHODOXY: INSTITUTIONAL CHRISTIANITY

Some people who seek a better way to live (and are attracted to Jesus' teachings), a healthier psychology (and find sense in Paul's theology), and like living in community (and like John's unifying message), *but are not mystics*. Could a nonmystic find a place in the Jesus movement? Mystics and other deeply religious people found in Jesus, Paul, and John what they needed. Those who wanted to be deeply religious, but were less inclined to have the emotional foundation for the radical life of faith (in other words, they were less emotional about life, sometimes numb or depressed, or sometimes just highly intellectual or habitual), needed a way to feel a part of the movement. They could, however, find deep meaning in rites and rituals. In response, Christianity began offering sacraments, orders of worship, and a prescribed set of correct beliefs (orthodoxy). It gave thinkers a way to feel deeply religious in their own way, not just in the mystics' more emotional way. The mystic feels Jesus' ethical mysticism, Paul's mystical union, or John's loving God without the need for trappings and orthodoxy. The mystic experiences eternal life from now on. The nonmystic thinks about life, but doesn't feel it so easily. If the Church didn't offer something tangible that would make sense to the nonmystics, they would be deeply jealous and definitely left out, so the Church offered them a place if they would affirm the right beliefs, follow the right path, and participate in the mysteries of the sacraments.

At its best, orthodoxy is about the same kind of "happy obedience" that the Jews teach. In Quakerism it is called "living the testimonies." For those who prefer the world of thought, it is a way to feel good about their connection to their religious community. It's a place for thinkers in the mystical world of feelers. Some of the greatest theological thinkers come from this place.

At its worst, orthodoxy finds in Jesus, Paul, and John rules that must be followed. These are the Church leaders who substitute a new law for the old law, and this new law is just as punitive and restrictive as the old one. This is the way of biblical inerrancy that overlooks the spirit of the law for legalism.

Sports teams are an excellent example of the integration of orthodoxy into the free-flowing nature of the game. On a good sports team a few players play the game intuitively and easily, but most players have to develop the right moves and techniques through hours of practice and repetition. These less-talented players need structure, roles, and even rituals to fit well into the team. A good coach knows how to let the talented, free-flowing players break from the fundamental patterns, and how to keep the less talented, less intuitive players in the right place at the right time. In other words, both mystical athletes and orthodox athletes exist. Together they can make up an excellent team.

However, we see just as many teams with coaches who squelch all freedom in favor of all their players playing only a set role. Talented, intuitive players might learn from such a system, but in the long run, they have to join another team with which their talents can be unleashed. These kinds of team are examples of orthodox legalism, which is what Jesus began his ministry protesting against.

In summary, Jesus, standing up against orthodox legalism, offered us an ethical mysticism; Paul offered a mystical reconciliation by faith; and John offered a mystical communion. Orthodoxy then offered a place for those who needed rites and rituals to help them feel the divine. Jesus taught a way to live, Paul taught a way to be at peace, John taught a way to find community, and orthodoxy provided a structure for community.

At this point we see that we have circled the theological spectrum. When community becomes restrictive to the point of legalism, it loses its sense of community. So a protest against legalism leads to those who follow a new ethical mysticism, those who find healing in a mystical union, those who experience the love of God in community, and those who enjoy a happy obedience with civility, good manners, and shared rites and rituals. It is the revolving nature of community—the revolution of community.

WHAT DIFFERENCE DOES THIS MAKE?

The early Church would not have gone anywhere, would not have grown and developed, if it had not developed communities. The breadth of theological perspectives within the early Church lent itself to community building. When Jesus came onto the public stage, Judaism was a community breaking down, caught up in legalism. What Jesus offered was a renewal movement—liberation from legalism and its oppressiveness. That in itself was significant, but Paul helped the Jesus movement open its doors and become truly inclusive. His theology of grace that flows through faith, and his assertion that Jesus was the Christ—a union or reconciliation of God with humankind— helped people learn to be open with one another, which is a necessary ingredient to community. Then John lifted up the idea of the existence of an overarching goodness, a loving and sacrificial God that makes community great. Finally, the Church found a way to open its doors to nonmystical, less emotional people by developing a mythology and rites and rituals and gentle rules. These trappings and rules, as long as they were of service to the community, helped to sustain community. Of course, the very rules that once sustained community also would become a new stage for legalism that would rob community of its life.

Quakerism, as much as any other religious sect, has tried to focus on community. The "sense of the meeting" is very, very important. Without this deep and abiding trust that the community will find the right way, even if it is slow and laborious, Quakers, as with all religious sects, fall into legalism. It doesn't just depend on trusting the community, though. It also depends on affirming those who are ethical mystics, those who seek a transforming openness, those who feel the love of God, and those who find joy in following the testimonies. Embracing these varieties of "Christian" expressions is vital to community life.

A few years ago a renewal movement occurred in Quakerism called the New Foundation Fellowship. Lead by the late Lewis Benson, this movement sought to reemphasize George Fox's focus on the Light of *Christ.* Benson believed that Quakers had turned away from Christ and thereby lost some of their early strength. The trouble with the movement, however, was that many of its disciples were adamant that Quakers *had* to be Christ-centered, which many Quakers are not. They had fallen into legalism. Thus, though the objective of the movement was to renew Quakerism, it became divisive instead. You had to be either on their side or against them.

Communities don't work that way. Communities embrace differences. Differences in community are grounds for dialogue. Hegel (in Lavine, 1984) was right: a spirit of community exists that loves to hear an antithesis to the thesis, for out of disagreement and dialogue comes a synthesis—a new and better idea. This is exactly what the Quaker idea of "continuing revelation" is about.

The magnetism of early Christianity was not built on the creation of exclusive, self-centered communities but on inclusive, radically trans- forming, liberating communities. What Jesus began was a movement that lifted up the celebration of life within community as well as the sacrificial nature of love. He didn't distinguish who was welcome and who would be excluded. He opened himself up to people who felt ex- cluded—children and adults alike—and began a movement that of- fered diverse and different people a place to belong. Paul expanded that inclusiveness into the Greco-Roman world with a theology that was built on openness—openness of mind, or heart, to people and es- pecially to God. John wrote beautifully about the love of God that shed new light on a dark world, expressed in a community of loving and gracious people. His theology was built on love that accepts and calls people to active love that is the fulfillment of God's love. The Church itself was created so that people would not be excluded. By creating rites and rituals, room for all was created—even the thinkers who might not *feel* the same way as Paul and John.

Although no community exists that does not exclude, certainly some standards for inclusion are more conducive to building commu- nity than others. Early Christianity has four great examples of such standards, and its principles were based on celebration of life, sacrifi- cial love, openness, and a community touched by the love of God. These are principles of inclusion for those who would seek a life touched by love. Those excluded are those who are caught in the web of hatred and life-negating activities. They are not, though, excluded because they are different, because they are odd, or because they doubt or question. Such reasons are not grounds for exclusion from true community. Early Christianity offers us a way to develop com- munity that is an affirmation of life. The only people excluded from this way of life are those who find no way to affirm life, choosing rather to negate life through the propagation of hate or life-destroying behavior.

The Revolution of Community

Communities are revolutionary. I use the word *revolution* for two reasons. First, communities revolve similar to a spiral. They are born out of renewal, nurtured by openness and love, develop testimonies or gentle rules of behavior, then get swallowed up in legalism, only to be renewed in some advanced form again. Second, communities are so incredibly life-giving that they feel revolutionary. They transform lives and political circumstances as does nothing else. Communities give Life!

Why are communities so often countercultural? Because in community we find a very effective way to enhance and nurture radical ideas, and true communities always hold up life-giving perspectives and behavior that our dominant cultures just cannot do. Being part of true community gives life.

In the history of how the early Church developed is a template for the development, the revolving nature of, and the revolutionary life-giving power of true community. It is both difficult and simple: seek the spirit of the law, open up to God or the Christ or the Light, let the love of God blossom with those we are with, and be good.

Chapter 9

Challenging the Powers: A Revolutionary Pseudocommunity

In the revolving nature of communities the inherent pitfall centers around power, which is usually expressed through either institutionalization or seeking to win. To the latter expression of power I now turn.

During the 1970s schools all over the nation were designated as "magnet" schools. They were schools set in inner-city neighborhoods with innovative programs, usually based on an "open education" philosophy, that were meant to attract diverse parents who wanted their children to receive excellent and innovative education in an integrated environment. For a while these schools were very successful in many places.

We found such a school when we moved to Memphis in 1985: Springdale Memphis Magnet School, where we enrolled our children. From the start it was obvious that this was an exceptional school. Teacher morale was high. The administration was efficient. Students were learning. Parents were very involved.

My wife, Susan, had been deeply involved in open education for a number of years, teaching in open-ed schools in New York City, visiting open-ed schools in England, and teaching open ed to prospective teachers at a Connecticut college. For a year I had worked with her in a day care center and had learned about open ed as well. Most of our experience, however, had been in private, early-childhood settings. We had not seen how open ed could or would work within the more strictly defined atmosphere of the public schools.

Although the goals and objectives of open education are common to most educational philosophies, open education operates quite differently.

© 2006 by The Haworth Press, Inc. All rights reserved.
doi:10.1300/5653_10

- Rather than desks and teacher-directed activities, open-ed class-rooms are composed of learning centers with children choosing their educational interests.
- Rather than children working with little interaction with other children, open ed encourages children to choose to either work alone or with their friends and peers.
- Rather than teachers directing the learning curriculum, open-ed teachers function more as resource persons for the children. They organize the learning activities, partnering with the children.
- Rather than parents being primarily involved through parent-teacher organizations, fund-raising, and overseers of homework, open-ed parents are expected to volunteer to participate in the classroom learning experiences.
- Rather than homework being an academic norm, open-ed en-courages children to play after school, lifting up the value of play for children.

A typical day in an open-ed classroom would consist of a group gathering time to begin the day, with singing and children sharing with one another their daily experiences and what they learned. The teacher would describe the learning centers, and release the children to choose which of them they would like to participate in. Throughout the day each child would be expected to work at each learning center, but the children are given ample time to spend the majority of their day at their favorite centers working on pet projects.

Sometimes a number of children become interested in a particular subject and want to really dig into it. I once volunteered to show the movie *Gandhi* to my son's class. The students became quite fasci-nated with it, so the teacher decided to develop a curriculum around India and that period of history. She created a geography center fo-cused on India; a sociology center on the culture and religions of In-dia; a history center focused on Gandhi's influence on Martin Luther King Jr.; a math center comparing the monetary systems of India, Great Britain, and the United States; a science center focused on In-dian weather; and a reading center filled with books on Gandhi and India. It was quite interesting. I was impressed with what the children learned.

Springdale had thrived under the strong leadership of a principal who embraced and understood open education. She not only kept the curriculum true to open-ed philosophy, she also kept the school board from interfering with its usual demands for uniformity. The school was truly a magnet for parents seeking to be involved in innovative education. In a city in which segregated schools were the norm, Springdale Memphis Magnet School was well mixed racially and ethnically, without busing, despite being in a nearly all African-American, poor neighborhood.

But Springdale was two schools in one. We had two different types of classrooms. One wing of the school was open ed, the other wing was what we called "traditional education"—with desks in rows and teacher-directed curricula. The traditional wing was essentially a neighborhood school, with children coming from the depressed, poverty-stricken neighborhood surrounding the school. These kids performed poorly in school, few of their parents were involved in the school, and most of the school's discipline problems were among these children. So one wing was well integrated, filled with parents who were involved in their children's education, and for the most part were middle class and doing well. The other wing was filled with deeply disadvantaged, almost all African-American, inner-city kids from mostly single-parent homes. We coexisted together in a sort of segregation between middle class and poverty class. It was a mirror of our larger society, but still possessed an avenue of escape from both poverty and segregation. Somehow, despite the school's inherent contradiction, our principal, teachers, and parents held it together with great pride.

Then the principal died of cancer. In her place a new principal was brought in who had her own ideas about how the school should operate. Although this new principal had been successful at another school, she did not appear to embrace and understand open ed. Soon the atmosphere at the school became strained with grumbling teachers. Rumors began to surface that the principal was trying to dismantle open ed, that the school board had only tolerated the prior principal and had placed the new principal at Springdale to change it to a more traditional and acceptable approach to education. The summer after her first year at Springdale, these rumors ran rampant among the white parents, and a massive white flight from the school occurred.

By the time September rolled back around only a few white parents were left among the parents committed to sustaining open education. My wife and I were two of those few, but I had to face a fact that I had not previously noticed. Almost all of my friends had left the school. I had thoughtlessly befriended only white parents. I was not as liberal minded as I had thought.

Owning up to our fallacies is not a bad thing. It is humiliating, but if one can take the initial embarrassment, it leads to humility—one of those great, traditional Christian virtues. After a period of embarrassment, I was able to reach out to those whom I had unconsciously shunned, and new friends, who happened to be African American, came just as easily because of our common interests. Our children were working and playing together, and we wanted them to be raised with good values and a good education.

Our new principal was bothered by the split between the two schools in one. She often talked about making the traditional school program as good as the open-ed program. What I think she did not realize was that it was the middle-class backgrounds of those in the Magnet School that lifted up the children's interest in education. Accompanying my admission that I had lived a social life based on prejudice was a revelation that race and ethnic differences were not the only factors that divided us. Class differences became obvious to me. It wasn't pretty, but I could see that what helped make the magnet school so good was that the children from the magnet school had parents who were expecting their children to learn in school. Children in the traditional school were living down to their parents' low expectations and poor attitudes about education. The two schools in one was a mirror of two segregated socioeconomic classes. Any principal entering such a school would be concerned with this conflict.

My wife and I were part of a large group of parents who thought that the principal was undermining what had been a wonderfully successful school. I could see that she was not really studying open-ed appropriately, and the open-ed teachers were being left unprotected from the demands the school board placed on traditional teachers that our previous principal had shielded them from (so that they could focus on a different way of teaching).

Tension mounted, until open-ed teachers could not fully hide their discouragement from volunteer parents. They were obviously worried, upset, and trying not to complain to parents, but it gradually seeped out. They were very upset with the principal's leadership.

We created a working group of parents to try to revitalize open ed, and after a series of confusing and conflict-filled meetings a number of us became convinced that our principal was not doing her job. In response, we decided to deepen our understanding of open ed so that we could better articulate what we wanted, and we decided as well to create a marketing plan for our school to help get its magnetism back.

My wife, who has a master's degree in early childhood education and was trained in open ed, wrote an essay that articulated the philosophy of open ed that was passed around among parents. In addition, a group of us traveled to Jackson, Mississippi, to visit a magnet school similar to ours. We returned with a wealth of ideas and enthusiasm. Our vision of what we wanted was becoming much clearer. We also created the design for a flyer and began toying with ideas about how to get the city's newspaper to write about our school program. In the meantime, though, morale among teachers was deteriorating rapidly. A couple of our best teachers quit, and instead of focusing on the positive vision we were developing, we became angry.

A community organizer from the Industrial Areas Foundation (IAF), Gerald Taylor, had been sent to Memphis on request from some church leaders who wanted help organizing people to lift up the oppressed in the city and help them get some political power. Some in our group were acquainted with this charismatic organizer and believed he could help us create an action plan. I asked him to come to one of our parent meetings, and he promised to meet with us if I could get fifteen parents to come to the meeting. I called twenty parents, and eighteen of them said they'd definitely come. Gerald came to the meeting, and his presence and ideas immediately mobilized us into action. We left that meeting not only positive about what we could do, but also awed by his dynamic leadership. For the first time in my life, I truly understood what community organizers are capable of. He was helping us to mobilize our impotent anger into powerful action by helping us truly work together.

Over the next half year our group became so well-organized and active that the school board was forced to listen to us. We also became great friends with one another. Unfortunately, despite our accomplishments the school had torn apart and had truly lost its magnetism.

In spite of our efforts, open ed was trashed. We became great friends, but lost the battle.

Every week we talked, planned, engaged in actions, and spent time in the classrooms with our children. A number from our group became deeply involved in larger activities of the IAF—called Shelby County Interfaith (SCI)—and at least three received intensive training in community organizing from the IAF. Similar to other communities, we became fast friends who, despite mostly going our separate ways over the ensuing years, still delight at chance meetings when we can catch up on our lives since those days and remember the spirit of community that we had together.

For me that community truly taught me how to live a life unafraid of diversity. After recognizing my unconscious prejudice during those early days of white flight from the school, I found a new community that taught me that it is orientation to life that matters much more than race or ethnicity. I will forever appreciate how liberating and life transforming that was for me.

But why did we lose the battle for Springdale? That question has vexed me for many years. Until recently I have been somewhat unwilling to admit what was wrong with our group. Although we were a self-contained community with all of the life-giving nature of community, we had a dark reason for our existence that hurt our effort. We had an enemy—the principal. As I reflect on that I can now see that an element of exclusivity existed in our group that meant that we could accept only those who agreed with our assessment of what was wrong at the school (which limited our ability to grow) and that we were more interested in power and victory than in cooperation and transformation. In some ways we were similar to a fundamentalist church group that is built upon the demand for right belief and the identification of an enemy. Such groups become self-contained, cause major problems, and are eventually shoved aside as irrelevant and out of touch. That is essentially what happened to us.

During those years when our children were at Springdale, partly because I helped to create a Gandhi curriculum, I studied Gandhian methods of creating change. Two characteristics that Gandhi adhered to stood out that we avoided. One was that although Gandhi understood that seeking to change systems meant that an adversary in fact existed, when his organizations were able to gain the advantage in their battles—when they suddenly had more power than their adversaries—he backed off. He used to say that it is not right to pressure one's adversary from a position of advantage. For more traditional power brokers, this was incredible. They would protest, "But now we can crush them! We are right on the edge of total victory!" Gandhi would reply that the fact that you can crush them is all the more reason to back off implying that we are not in this to hurt our adversary. We are in this to gain power over our *own* lives *and* to gain true friendship with our adversary. We want to make it so that they do not see us as their enemy. Unfortunately, our group was unable to ever see the principal as anything other than an enemy. I now believe that our view of her poisoned the school as much as her inadequacies ever did.

Another Gandhian principle was that a high degree of civility should be practiced in all confrontations. Gandhi insisted that activists who worked for his causes treat their enemies with great politeness and respect, even while demanding equal respect. This meant that nonviolent activists would have to be as inoffensive in as many of their ways as possible—from how they ate, to how they dressed, to how they behaved.

However, early in our group's activities Gerald told us that this would not be a place for politeness. It was about power, and it would get ugly. He said that politeness is the bane of the middle class—the main reason why they are unable to break into places of power. With this idea in mind, we were highly confrontational, sometimes to the point of rudeness. We believed we had to be this way, but I no longer see it that way. I think it alienated us from those whom we were asking to work with. Without civility and politeness, how can people truly work together? Those we were fighting learned from our harshness that they didn't really want to work with us. We created our own exclusion. We were strong enough to force them to listen to us, but they didn't want us to stay. They didn't see us as interested in friendship, which meant that in order to protect the larger school system, they had to win and we had to lose. In other words, we had a community that was inwardly friendly but outwardly unfriendly. We bred our own destruction.

Can a revolutionary community create a truly new way? At Springdale we did not find the way, but I believe that Gandhi did show such a way. For a community to truly change its circumstances—and not just replace one power-hungry administration with another—it must have an eye for friendship, which means backing off at the point of having gained the advantage (so that the adversary does not get hurt, scared, and angry in return) and being highly civil, respectful, and kind. This might slow the charge down, but in the long run, it is the only way to truly share power.

Abraham Lincoln once told an angry northern senator who was speaking to him about annihilating his southern enemies as the Civil War was ending, "The best way to destroy an enemy is to make him your friend." We befriended one another within our activist group, but we were unable to befriend—and thus destroy—our enemy. Because of that, we lost the battle.

We were, in fact, a closed community, which became our own demise. A true community—one that gives life to all who encounter it—is an open community. It is about civility, friendship, respect, and peacefulness. It might have to fight for respect and power, but a true community is more interested in friendship than in power over another.

This is the basic reason why fundamentalism does not create true community. Fundamentalism in any religious or social form is based upon rigidity, uniformity, and having an enemy. It is not friendly with faith that means openness. Instead, it has a prescribed set of beliefs that its members must affirm. Those who question those beliefs are not acceptable. Thus, fundamentalism discourages questioning and free speech.

Fundamentalism may look diverse, but it is actually no friend of true diversity. Because its members adhere to a basic, unquestionable belief system, members create a single cultural ethos that leaves no room for cultural openness.

Finally, it has an automatic scapegoat. Those who not fully agree are not just outsiders, they are enemies. Having a mutual enemy is an easy way to manage anxiety. Because anxiety is fear without an object, finding an enemy creates an object for fear. Fear is easier to cope with than anxiety, for it gives the group a way to fight. You can't fight anxiety—you just learn to manage it. You can fight the object of fear, however.

Try as I'd like, I can no longer deny that our Springdale group was a fundamentalist group. We had the potential to be a true community, but we became open-ed fundamentalists instead. We had a single belief system—that open ed as we defined it was exactly and without compromise what we should have. We demanded strict adherence to a confrontational strategy that was harsh and impolite, and we saw the principal as an enemy to get rid of—not as someone with whom we could befriend.

Certainly elements of good existed in our group, just as they exist in all fundamentalist groups, but we were guilty of the very thing we were fighting. In seeking to stop an abuse of power (which was destroying the school), we abused those in power. We created irreconcilable differences. A true community doesn't do this. True communities create friendships, even when they have to cause change first.

Yet I can still see that from the original core of powerless and discouraged parents that some truly affirming empowerment grew from among us. Those who learned from SCI how to create alliances that empowered the powerless took that knowledge with them into all sorts of arenas. Some were able to organize grassroots community programs that have given hope to children and their parents. Some created inner-city church ministries that are true lights to the city. Some used the organizational knowledge to pull together diverse people to accomplish great things.

The key for those who found ways to apply those insights was that we all on some intuitive level realized the pitfalls of fundamentalism. As we moved on in our lives we took some of those organizational skills that Gerald taught us, and, instead of blending it with rigidity, impoliteness, and finding enemies, we blended it with openness, dialog, friendliness, and peaceful cooperation.

Over the years I have met many peaceful, community-minded people who describe early experiences in fundamentalist groups. Many of them were involved in the Jesus movement of the 1960s and 1970s. They left the movement for the same reasons I let go of our Springdale group—they finally understood the weakness of fundamentalism. What they took with them from those experiences was similar to what I took with me—knowledge of what was good about community as evidenced within that group. Inwardly we were, for a short time, open, flexible, civil, and peaceful. We erred in not letting those higher values determine our outward actions. As we matured and left such groups, though, we could and often did find ways to reconcile the inward with the outward, taking that openness, flexibility, and peacefulness with us in all our actions. We may have come from flawed groups, but what we learned when we admitted those flaws made us better people.

Chapter 10

A Championship Basketball Team

For some, the idea of not having an enemy naturally means that competitive athletic teams are pseudocommunities. Not in my mind, though. Because I believe a great difference exists between competition against and competition with, I coach teams to learn a deeper level of respect for their opponents. The following is an example.

In the fall of 2001 I was assigned a team of high school basketball players for a church league of seventeen- and eighteen-year-old boys. I asked a friend of mine, Marcus Tate, to be my assistant coach. Marcus is a man of great relationship intelligence, very likeable, who had never coached before. He wanted to learn what coaching was about.

In our league is a rule that all players must play for 50 percent of every game they are at. That means that if you have a particularly good player—one who can dominate play—it is best to have less than ten players so he can play more than the rest. I have found that the ideal number of players in our league is seven. It is easy to rotate seven players around so that they all get some rest and the best can be in the game when needed.

Unfortunately, we were assigned ten players. Two of them, Mario and Roman, were superior players who could dominate a game. I would only be able to play them half the game. The problem that loomed, then, was that these two key players could be upset with their playing time and contaminate the team chemistry. At our first practice, after we watched the players scrimmage, recognizing that we had mostly average players with above-average quickness, I reminded them that the 50 percent play rule would mean no one would get to play more than half of any game. I suggested that the way to cope with it would be to play a very fast-paced game, applying full-court pressure

doi:10.1300/5653_11   93

constantly, rotating players in and out often. They agreed, and we went to work developing a disciplined press and understanding our offensive strengths and weaknesses.

By January we were known as a team that played a highly intense game with constant pressure. We coached them to push the pace at all times, and, in turn, I found two compatible teams of five players—Mario on one team and Roman on the other—and rotated them in and out of the game in two minute intervals. That way every player would return to the game before he could cool down.

Three dynamics began to emerge. First, early in almost every game our opponent would adjust to our press, break it down, and take the lead—sometimes in double digits. In response, players would come back to the bench and exclaim, "We have to call off the press. They're killing us!" But I saw something different. I saw a team that was breaking our press while also getting frustrated and tired of it. Our team was executing very well, hustling and making adjustments that were close to causing turnovers. I believed that it was just a matter of time until the other team got a little sloppy with their passes, and we would come back. So I would respond, "No, it's not working yet, but it will. They are starting to break down." Inevitably, halfway through the third quarter (in all but one game) that is what would happen. Our opponent would get sloppy or tired, and we would pull even, then ahead. We usually had a small lead going into the fourth quarter and then won running away that last quarter.

We were good, though, because all of the team had bought into the notion that team defense was our strength. One player, Jeff, believed he was an excellent defensive player. He did have good one-on-one technique, but he hardly ever knew where his teammates were, so he did not know how to get their help when he was up against a quick player, and he could not help his teammates when they needed it. He was my weak link. Early in the season much scoring happened around him. So I worked especially hard with him, teaching him how to play team defense, how to force a good player to go the direction he wanted him to go. Halfway through the season he figured it out. That was when our team jelled.

The second dynamic was that the team began to truly love playing with Mario and Roman. The two boys did things that excited everyone, and the other players became so vocal in their praise of the two stars that it kept Mario and Roman happy despite that they would have played much more on most of the other teams we played (who had seven or eight players). The team itself was keeping the stars happy. The community feeling had more power than our stars had talent to showcase. Of course, it didn't hurt that we were winning most of our games. Winning heals many team chemistry problems.

The third dynamic was that two players on each of the rotating fives, Calvin and Jesse, and Myron and Jeff, were great friends, big and strong or quick, and were vocal leaders. They would not allow the team to loaf or get discouraged when games were tough. They did not make most of the big plays—Mario and Roman did—but they were inevitably on the floor wrestling for the ball and taking charges or getting rebounds. In addition, they never complained about their playing time. Since they were the true spiritual leaders of the team, others took their lead and followed the program without complaint. Calvin and Jesse in particular were the live wires, while Jeff and Myron knew how to play offense together better than any two on the team.

Part of the difficulty in creating a good team is convincing certain players that they must accept a limited role for the team to play its best (which was our transcendent vision—teamwork—another word for community). Most players dream of being the team star, but there are rarely more than two stars on a team. The stars have to be given the ball more often, given more freedom, and be in the game at key points. Role players have to be given a limited assignment that often makes their contribution obvious only to those who know the nuances of the game. I had four players who claimed a role by talent (Mario and Roman) and leadership ability (Calvin and Jesse). I had six players who had to accept limited roles. Gevon, Ben, and Floyd were great defensive players, as quick or fast as anyone in the league, and Gevon could shoot well if he was wide open, but basically their roles were to disrupt the other team's offense. I spent a lot of time complimenting their defensive abilities until it was obvious that they were very proud to help the team in that way. Jeff and Austin were my most limited players, but after Jeff got motivated at playing team defense he became an incredibly happy leader on the team. Austin, our largest boy, played very rough and fouled out often. That roughness became what we needed from him. He fouled people trying to shoot layups so awkwardly (and unintentionally) that he discouraged them from shooting them. Both boys could also hit three-point shots in bunches, so I instructed their teammates to give them an immediate second shot if they hit their first one. Myron was the most cooperative player on the team, easily accepting his role as our main rebounder and scoring mostly on put backs.

Ben was a wildly active player who had one characteristic that threatened team chemistry. He hated to be taken out of the game, and would scowl when being removed. Coach Marcus, however, loved the way Ben played. He outhustled everyone on the court. Marcus was quite vocal at praising Ben, and we asked Ben to not complain with his playing time, reminding him that all players were playing the same amount. When he complied with our request, he ended all the team's complaints about playing time.

Meanwhile, Marcus and I were growing in respect for one another. I found in him an ability to excite the team as well as reinforce my strategy that made our work together very smooth. Our coaching chemistry was great.

By the end of the year we were aware that we had extraordinary team chemistry. We hung together extremely well during the rough spots in close games, the hardest thing for a team to do. When teams are out of rhythm, which happens to the best of teams a number of times during a game, it is very hard for players to not try too hard to do it all by themselves. We were excellent at staying cohesive until we regained our team rhythm.

We lost one game before the championship tournament, a loss that upset the boys much more than it did me. I knew that without that loss they would not understand that even good teams cannot take victory for granted. *Any* team can be beaten on any given day.

We were one of the two top seeds at the championship tournament to end the year. In our first game we got behind, pulled even, then ran the score up to about fifteen points. At that point, the team we were playing began playing a full-court press against us. It was only the second time all year we had been pressed, and we kept throwing the ball away. They kept scoring. We won the game by eight points, but it was obvious that they had uncovered our weakness. To beat a press a team has to play with some degree of deliberation, which we never did. I knew that if the other coaches saw what I did, we could be in trouble.

It was the championship game that truly tested our mettle.

We were playing a team with equal talent. They had quick players who worked hard and could score inside and outside. They also had a player who was about four inches taller and thirty pounds heavier than any of our players. We had beaten them twice in close games during the season, so their coach called them together for an extra practice the night before our game to learn how to break our press. He borrowed seven players from other teams and made his team break a press with seven players covering the floor on defense.

It worked. They pulled out a twelve point lead, and my players were begging me to call off the press. I certainly was tempted to, for I could see that the other team had more confidence than any other team we had encountered. But I also knew that my team had never done well in a half-court game with other teams. Our offense sprung off our defense and did best at a fast pace. I demanded that we stick with it and keep the pressure on.

Finally, halfway through the third quarter they lost their rhythm and we made a run. Their frustration began to show, our confidence and rhythm soared, and by the end of the quarter we were six points up. In the fourth quarter the other team could not do anything right and we could not miss. They got further behind but never tried a full-court press to challenge our weakness. We won by twelve points— a twenty-point swing.

We knew we had done something special, because we had won as a team, not because our most talented players dominated the game. Every player on our team had something to brag about—a steal, a blocked shot, a clutch shot, a charge taken. We placed four players on the all-tournament team, but the best part was the reaction of players such as Floyd, Jeff, and Myron. They soaked it up like dry sponges. They did not want to go home. They knew, and I knew, that this was a special team, one that was more than just a team. We were a community.

After the game adults served pizza and soda to both teams, and we mingled together respectfully and happily. It had been a good game, we all knew, and their team was as gracious in defeat as ours was humble in victory—which was the way our pregame prayer had been worded. Both teams had developed a profound respect for one another, and it showed in the game itself and in the friendliness after the game.

Some teams are unable to find such graciousness and humility, partly because their leaders are unable to discern the difference between winning and doing one's best. I find it unfortunate that the dominant ethos of coaching today is one that encourages yelling, baiting the referees, and an overemphasis on winning. Such a style becomes almost completely focused on talent and authority—not on community. Teams that become true communities, however, do not have abusive, authoritarian coaches. They might not even win, although they inevitably win more than they lose, because team chemistry is very hard to beat. And it certainly is unforgettable.

I still see many of those young men from that team, and we immediately break into a smile. We talk about basketball, about what we are up to now, and about where their old teammates are. At some point in our conversation we mention our championship and exclaim, "We sure did have a special team, didn't we?"

The next year, Myron and Jeff played on an extraordinarily talented team that was highly favored to win the championship. In the semifinals they had a bad game, though, and unlike our team they were not able to pull together as a team and pull themselves out of the hole. Their stars tried to take over alone. The other team double-teamed them, and they lost. It was a powerful reminder to me of the incredible strength of community. Teams can often do better than pure talent alone. As I talked with Myron and Jeff after their loss, we commented on the many factors that gave the team success the year before and on what had happened with their new team.

It is strange: communities (or teams) are so fragile to build, but once they are built, they are virtually invulnerable. They sustain their members through struggles that individuals just cannot negotiate through with half the grace and ease as they can when surrounded by community.

Chapter 11

Professional Community

Community building has some practical aspects to it that the following community experience lifts up.

In the 1978 movie *Same Time, Next Year* Alan Alda and Ellen Burstyn play two married people caught up in a once-a-year affair with each other at the same location. Although the premise of the story—that an extramarital affair could enhance their lives without contaminating their mutual marriages—is deeply mistaken, the essence of the story was the year-by-year deepening of their history and love for each other. This essence is an essential truth in our experiences in community life. When we share an annual common encounter that is free of complications and immorality, we grow to care deeply and experience communion with one another.

In 1985 I attended my first Southeast Region meeting of the American Association of Pastoral Counselors (AAPC) at the Kanuga Conference Center in Hendersonville, North Carolina. At this writing I have been back there every year for twenty years. For me, Kanuga, as we usually call it, is a community experience. How it became a community experience is important to understand.

For the first two or three years I went to Kanuga I did not feel part of the comradery that was evident among longtime attendees. I kept returning because of the continuing education it offered me, the chance to enjoy the Appalachian Mountains, and the growing number of friends I was developing. In 1988 I was invited to join a working committee. I was surprised that our first order of business together was a sharing or "connecting" time. We were invited to tell personal stories and what was going on in our current lives. Such sharing lends itself to the discovery of point of commonality. It was in the working committee that I first found community at Kanuga. Of course, it was

doi:10.1300/5653_12   *99*

short-lived. Three days later we all went back home, but there was a sense that we would reconnect "same time next year."

The next year brought some of the old faces as well as some new ones, but the pattern continued to grow and deepen. I would return each year to find a larger group of friends with whom I had a longer sense of history. At the same time we were all participants in a shared vocational endeavor. We were pastoral counselors together. We knew firsthand what one another's work was—our difficulties and our joys. We were truly comrades in the same high calling and struggle to do good work and earn a living. Helping one another with this high calling was our shared transcendent vision.

Another joyful aspect of our time together was surprising to me. Because we had automatic vocational respect for one another, had a common sense of morality, *and* we were only in one another's presence for three to four days at a time, we could cut up in outrageous ways. We could dance and sing and joke and tell stories and laugh together in ways that were deeply relieving for professionals used to acting in a proper manner.

At Kanuga I often found myself experimenting with being less inhibited. My friends would give me honest, good-natured feedback. I could try out bolder behaviors, for no one would "tell on" me, worry about it, or be particularly offended. After all, people can tolerate a lot of tomfoolery when together only a few days! It was training in how to be a bolder, freer adult, how to be a leader.

Others were experimenting with new ways of being as well. For the most part I found their lack of inhibitions and openness refreshing, but there were, of course, some who rubbed me the wrong way. I am sure I rubbed some the wrong way as well. I often have been grateful that we spent only a few days a year together, for it is easy to tolerate certain behaviors or grating personalities for a short while. We did not need to work out some of the issues we would have needed to had we been with one another more often or longer. I have no doubt that some people were glad to see me only once a year, too. But we did not have to nor could we, given the time restraints, iron out personality problems. Tolerance was the key. I could greatly enjoy most folks, and tolerate a few others. In that way I learned how valuable and important toleration is.

I had some experiences with intolerable behavior. Occasionally a person would get caught engaged in immoral behavior or have to be confronted about living too close to the edge of what has been called "the forbidden zone." Most of such behavior was about sexual indiscretion. In particular, we sometimes had to oust a member who engaged in immoral and illegal sexual activity with a client. Such behavior was not only wrong according to our ethical standards, but it threatened our whole association. It was often very difficult to deal with such occurrences, for it meant that a person we had become friends with would probably not be seen again in pastoral counseling circles. It was sad.

For the most part, though, such indiscretions were rare, and after a period of confrontation and reeducation, we were able to lift up our ethical standards in a stronger and more influential way. That helped us maintain the relaxing, joyful nature of our time together at Kanuga.

As I've grown older, as our years together have mounted up, I have been called upon to share the responsibilities for the creation of that community atmosphere. Now I see that the elders who spoke so longingly of Kanuga and their friends when I was a new, young pastoral counselor were opening their arms to me, drawing me in, and seeking to discern my gifts and help me find a working place in the community. Sometimes we call this "recruitment," but it is more. It is a nurturing community.

The leaders of the community must attend to the sustenance of a community. My Kanuga experience was about being welcomed, drawn in, accepted, taught, and called into leadership. It is a blueprint for community building worth looking in depth at.

My assimilation and participation in the community we had at Kanuga occurred in stages: hospitality, discernment of gifts, opportunities for shared work, learning to think differently and be different, and the call to leadership.

HOSPITALITY

A community cannot be sustained unless it is conscientious about being hospitable to those who visit. If visitors are not drawn into the community, the passage of time and the death of its members will kill the community. A community must have new blood so that as old members die or move away new members can take their place in leading and nurturing the community.

At one point in our life together we noticed that hardly any of our members were young anymore. Our numbers were dwindling, our hairs were grayer. As we discussed this phenomenon we realized that we deeply missed the energy, curiosity, and youth culture that was so obvious when we had a good number of young pastoral counselors in our midst, and we also recognized a deep yearning within ourselves to teach those who are younger how to do the work. Without young people present we would have no one to pass on our body of knowledge and wealth of experience. We older folks needed that as much as younger folks might want it. We desperately needed to keep the breadth of ages strong at Kanuga.

We set goals for ourselves to recruit new members. To accomplish this goal we knew that we had to put our money behind our goals, so we established and carefully administered a scholarship program for first-time attendees. We carefully tracked their registrations and sought to make them feel welcome by encouraging longtime attendees to reach out to them and welcome them. We brought in some of the nation's best speakers for our plenaries. We sought to find out what interests and skills they might have so that we could nominate them for committee positions. We created fun, recreational times. In short, we tried to help them feel at home and welcomed.

Another particularly interesting reality that we have begun to face is that we have stopped trying to make the way easier, acknowledging instead that the path to becoming a pastoral counselor is very difficult, expensive, and at the end, doesn't always pay that well. In telling prospective pastoral counselors this truth we have begun to lift up the real reason why we love this profession: it is a high calling to help people find meaning in their lives and wisdom from their suffering. It is deeply meaningful work. We're not in it for the money.

We were letting them in on the real reason why we came back to Kanuga every year—for support and encouragement. The truth has long been that little makes this work easier, but community lightens the load. The difference between hard work and toil is that communities make hard work just hard work. Doing it alone is beyond hard, it is toil.

Hospitality is not so much about creating a relaxing, easy atmosphere as it is about creating a place where one can find renewal, encouragement, and support. In many cases this does not mean a vacation, but an accepting and challenging environment. Kanuga has been such a place. It is a beautiful Appalachian Mountain retreat, but the programs and activities we do are not just meant to be easy. They are also meant to send us back to our work with new tools and insights, greater commitment, and a deeper hope. For it is the seeking of hope that much of pastoral counseling is truly about, and hope is found by searching. Hospitality at Kanuga has been mainly about joining with new people in their searches.

DISCERNMENT OF GIFTS

Communities must know their members well enough to not only discern how each member is gifted, but also to help lift up that gift. A prevalent attitude in the pastoral counseling community that is that every person is gifted. Much of the work of a pastoral counselor is helping clients not only find hope, but it also includes the affirmation of the client's unique gift. I had a supervisor, Jay Stearnes, who was a master at finding something in his clients that he truly respected. Whenever he referred a client to me, he usually talked only briefly about pathology or diagnosis. Most of what he told me was the gift he perceived in the person. It always made me want to meet the client, for it made the person special.

Kanuga was filled with many people similar to Jay Stearnes—people who sought the gift within that commanded respect and made each person special. Plenty of new attendees did not find this respect, but plenty did. I was one. It was obvious to me from early on that people were glad I was present, and a few seemed truly interested in me and my gifts. Such affirmation encourages one to open up. It encourages one to share more, to be vulnerable and real. Without such openness a community is crippled.

One of the greatest deterrents to community is the difficulty some have towards accepting diversity—cultural, religious, or political diversity. At Kanuga I never encountered the community having difficulty with religious diversity. AAPC had long grown beyond the place where we were seeking to be just Christian, so we were open to all sorts of expressions of faith. We did have difficulties adjusting to the growth of the number of women and minorities in our ranks, and we are presently having difficulty accepting people with right-wing political ideologies. The good news is that there appears to be an ethic of openness that makes us question our own ideologies and assumptions. Men struggled with the different ways of thinking and governing that women wanted, but we struggled with an openness to it that allowed women to feel welcomed enough to join. People of color are finding the same dynamic of resistance, openness, and acceptance, and I believe we will learn to accept political differences better. What we will not accept, however, is closed-mindedness and bigotry, for those are poisons to community. Even community acceptance has limits. Just as unethical behavior threatens community and must be made taboo, certain attitudes do as well and must be made inadmissible. Yes, a community orthodoxy—a set of "right beliefs" exists. It is not just about openness and acceptance, but also about civility and a willingness for bridges to be built from two directions. I may be able to accept your opposing opinion, but if you refuse to accept mine (for reasons other than seeing it as immoral) we cannot commune with each other. A mutual respect must be given for differences as well as for gifts. Gifts are, in fact, part of what make us different. Each gift is unique, truly different from another's gift. Discernment and respect for gifts is vital to community life.

OPPORTUNITIES FOR SHARED WORK

Maybe the best way to get to know someone is to work together. Learning to coordinate efforts and discern strengths, weaknesses, and talents is best done at work. That "work" can be play, such as dancing together or team athletics, and still be considered a form of work.

We had to maintain the integrity and attractiveness of an organization that supported more than five hundred regional members. Important, necessary work functions needed to be done in order to accomplish this maintenance, everything from highly intellectual work to manual labor. One year I oversaw a volunteer crew of four who gathered food, carried amplifiers, moved chairs, and ran errands. Another year I supervised the collection of short essays and worked with eight persons to edit them and bind them into a booklet. Each shared job gave us all the opportunity to appreciate one another's work styles and work ethics. Some would be prompt, others tardy. Some would make major contributions, others minimal. You can find points of compatibility (and incompatibility) quite easily when working together.

Every year I had another job and made new friends through our shared work. My history with an ever-broadening group of friends grew and grew. By now I have such a large group of friends at Kanuga that when I return next year, God willing, I will have a specific memory of shared work with someone nearly every place I go.

Shared work creates shared history.

LEARNING TO THINK DIFFERENTLY AND BE DIFFERENT

Every year I sit down with someone who understands people or community life from a completely different perspective than mine. Over the years I have come to appreciate what those with whom I disagree with give me as much or more than what those with whom I agree with give me. It's not that I find myself arguing, though, for an ethos exists in the Kanuga community that encourages us to find points of commonality. Just because someone had a differing point of view does not mean that we are not fundamentally concerned about the same problem. Our differences are in the solutions we believe are best, but our commonality is in our shared concern. Once we accept our shared concern, we inevitably can understand why we differ on solutions. Then it becomes a source of enjoyment to understand why we disagree, for the ensuing dialogue helps us find even better solutions to problems.

For years I have been a liberal Democrat. Lately I have found myself enjoying conversations with thoughtful conservatives more than just agreeing with another Democrat. When a conservative and I are able to talk respectfully and share our fundamental concerns and philosophies, I find myself being transformed by the talk. Sometimes it makes me feel more strongly that I am right; sometimes I decide I am wrong and change my mind. Dialogue is best among those who are willing to differ with respect. Kanuga offers a place where such dialogue is encouraged.

From this dialogue a movement has developed toward diversification. This process is different than just listening to different opinions. In fact, one might agree on nearly everything but still not find commonality because of cultural misunderstandings. We found that paying close attention to assumptions and sensitivities (or insensitivities) was more important than opinions. Much of what the white men had to do was based on having the grace to invite minorities to speak to them truthfully and critically and to be willing to change to accommodate those truths. What made it hard to change, though, was that it required sharing power. Leadership in the AAPC has long been—just as most corporations and associations in America have been—the privilege of white men. To invite new folks into the halls of power and prestige who have not long "waited their turn" (because they have not been allowed to be or have not been interested in being members for long) is difficult, but necessary if a community is truly interested in being diverse. It is a goal worth striving for, for our whole world is fast becoming diverse. Those institutions that are not diverse will increasingly become irrelevant.

We have been achieving diversification in AAPC in three steps. First, we have had to put our money where our mouths are. We provided many scholarships for women and minorities who needed financial help for training and to attend Kanuga. It was a major priority for us, and still is. Second, we encouraged a listening ethos and created structures and settings where deep listening could occur. We thought that the best way to draw persons into membership in our region was by listening to them. Third, we appointed and nominated women and minorities to positions of leadership, positions in which they could help to change how we operated. We are far from finished with this task—I'm not sure any community every finishes it—but we have embraced the process. I'm proud of that.

THE CALL TO LEADERSHIP

In any community are those who prefer to touch base with the core spirit of the community mostly as spectators as well as those who are drawn into the core leadership, who maintain the integrity of the community. A natural seasoning of leadership skills helps this latter group learn how to get things done.

We try to invite all returning Kanuga participants to join a committee in which the work of the AAPC is being done. If a person accepts nomination and is then elected to that committee, we find out quickly who the joiners are and who the spectators are. The spectators are those who come to about 50 percent of the meetings and contribute their thoughts and input at the meeting, but don't usually volunteer to do much of the follow-up work. They are still important to the committee work, because their ideas are often representative of many of our membership. The joiners are those who attend almost all of the meetings, volunteer to take responsibility for various tasks, and get the work done. When we find a person who does excellent work, the chair of the committee informs our leadership development committee—a nominating committee—which seeks to place that person in a position of greater responsibility.

We are not trying to rope people into work. In essence, the real purpose is to train excellent leaders. If a person is not personally interested in leadership or is not doing the jobs well, he or she will be naturally left off the slate of nominations for higher positions. That is, of course, unless we succumb to our prejudices and overlook some persons because of race, sex, or another blind spot, and we've certainly made such oversights.

Communities are not immune from the "isms." What makes communities different from institutional prejudice—prejudice that is built into the structure of the organization—is that communities are open to self-policing. Because we encourage dialogue and openness, we are more apt to face our prejudices before they become nominative.

I have seen the group face prejudices over and over again at Kanuga. It is that ethos of openness that creates the right check and balance to our human tribal instincts and insecurities. When we are truly open with one another we listen in new ways and learn of our points of commonality. The walls of prejudice break down.

As long as I return to Kanuga I will carry with me a desire to be myself, accept others as they are, be open with all, and enjoy the work and play. Enough of us return there with the same attitude to make me confident that Kanuga will continue to be a community experience for years to come.

Chapter 12

Dancing to Community

Historically, Quakers didn't dance. They did not even sing or allow music, at least not openly. However, though now Quaker, I grew up Methodist, and unlike the Baptists next door we could dance. I learned to love to dance—rock and roll, disco, jazz, and modern dance. I was not good at it, but I loved it. In fact, my wife, Susan, and I got to know each other during disco dances at the seminary I attended.

Susan once told me that she thinks dancing is peace work. It brings people together, helps them know and enjoy one another, and releases all sorts of pent up feelings. Modern Quakers, fortunately, are now quite fond of dancing, for we now see the sense in having peacefulness linked with joy.

Susan and I didn't dance much as we raised our two boys, until we were introduced to contra dancing a few years ago. There we rediscovered the joy of dance, and we also found a new community.

Contra is a type of dance that has evolved from early English-American dance, square dance, and swing dancing. Dancers begin in sets of four—a partner and a neighboring couple—dance for sixty-four counts to a simple pattern, then move or "progress" to another neighboring couple in the long line of dancers. Most of the bands play bluegrass music, jigs, and reels, but more and more of them are incorporating poly-rhythms and world drumbeats, transforming the dance from its "proper" beginnings to its present-day structured wildness.

When we arrived at our first dance we were quickly but patiently taught the fundamental moves and the basic choreography of the first dance. Then the music began and we danced. Each tune lasts ten to fifteen minutes, during which time one dances with everyone in the line. We quickly discovered that contra dance is not for couples with a tendency to be jealous.

doi:10.1300/5653_13

At that dance we were surprised not only by the vigor of the dance but also by the gracious acceptance of mistakes, especially by those who were excellent dancers. We suffered no snobbery or criticism. In fact, mistakes were treated with gentleness, smiles, and friendly laughter. I was often moved to the right place by friendly hands and arms. After the first dance, as I caught my breath and tried to apologize for the confusion I felt I had caused, a number of regular dancers spoke first. One asked me to dance the next one with her. Another told me I had done great for the first time. Another exclaimed with a smile, "In contra there are no mistakes—only creative moves."

By the end of the dance we were sure we would return. Not only had the group been fun and easy to be with, the dancing was relatively easy to learn, was loads of fun, and was very sensuous. We danced every other week for a couple of years, developing new friends and a sense of trust and joy that was totally unexpected. After each dance our friends Ernest and Joan would open their house up to dancers for a party of finger food, talk, and singing.

Something was deeply celebratory and life affirming about the dances. We felt a sense of transcendence at them that we could not get enough of. Clearly, we were not alone in these feelings, either. The community spirit that existed was great fun. (One evening as we were going out again, our then fifteen-year-old son, with the scornful smile of a wily teenager asked us, "Mom and Dad, are y'all getting a *life?*)

In time we began to hear about the national contra network and the dance weekend festivals some among us loved to attend. During the summer of 2001 Susan and I went to a Quaker conference in Asheville, North Carolina. While there we went to a dance at Warren Wilson College. As soon as we walked into the dance hall we were amazed at what was happening. The dance band, the Groovemongers, was playing music that was of a quality we had never heard at a dance before, and the dancers were moving to it in surprising ways with uncommon grace and creativity. Frankly, it was of such high quality we were a bit intimidated. Nonetheless, we joined in and found that the music was actually determining the quality of the dance. At nearly all of the dances we had participated in up until then we had never found the music to be that important. Mostly it was just about the dances and their choreography. But the Groovemongers were doing what Stevie Wonder (1976) once wrote that music has "a language we all understand . . . You can feel it all over." Their music was so excellent that they were making everyone better dancers. They made Susan and I better, too—no small feat!

After that awesome experience we soon joined others from Memphis in going to a weekend dance event in Knoxville, Tennessee. In Knoxville we were not only awed by the dancing, the atmosphere, and the music, we were also shocked that we could dance for fifteen hours in two days, leave exhausted, and immediately wish we could dance some more!

What we were finding was dancers with a rare combination of good moral boundaries (you could flirt and touch, but only while dancing, and only in the proper ways), gracious acceptance of one another's moves, strengths, and weaknesses, genuine appreciation of one another, and an opportunity to be very physical and sensuous.

Our caller, Martha Kelly, often exclaimed that she wanted us to have our own dance weekend. It had become clear to me why she said this: one reason was the joy of sharing our little dance community; the other would be the opportunity to draw our nontraveling dancers into a dance experience that could be beyond anything we experienced at our bimonthly dance. After Knoxville I too was convinced, so I called up the Groovemongers to check on their availability and fee. They were available on the dates we wanted, and their fee was quite reasonable. Immediately I began to campaign for a dance weekend and to poll our dancers to see if we might take up the challenge. There was obvious enthusiasm for the endeavor, so a few of the key leaders of the group agreed to meet to finalize an organizational plan for a dance weekend. Before the meeting, however, with the approval of our major natural leaders, I talked with the Groovemongers and we agreed that, upon final approval, they would come to Memphis for our weekend.

The meeting went exceptionally smoothly. Everyone wanted to do it, and as we looked at the financial projections it was clear that we had reason to be optimistic about its financial success. Just to be sure, though, about ten of us offered to donate money to the endeavor if we were to lose money. That was amazing to me. Not only had we coalesced enough to find a common activity, we were willing to make sacrifices for that cause. Nearly everyone at that gathering signed up to volunteer for one or two committees. Almost immediately our dance group began to grow.

We met every two or three weeks, often listening to the Groove-mongers' CD as we discussed business. We were careful to divide tasks into very manageable portions, reminding ourselves that our secondary goal was to make sure that no one did so much work that we could not enjoy the dancing. We hired an excellent caller, Seth Tepfer, from Atlanta, who was obviously very enthusiastic about coming. He passed out fliers everywhere he went, just as our "dance gypsies" (dancers who travel often to other dances) did.

Martha was seeing a dream of hers come true. She didn't have the energy or time to have done the work of organizing the weekend at that point in her life, so she took on her small portion and happily watched the smooth runnings of our group life. We were getting it done, and doing it very well.

Of course, our group struggled occasionally with our sense of unity and with the inevitable anxiety. We had some problems with hurt feelings, but, as coordinator of the event, I carefully reached out to those who felt slighted, seeking to let them know that I knew fully well how important they were. The group, though, was filled with members who followed up on my care with the "wounded" with their own embracing of one another. Obviously, the group wanted this to work without hurting anyone. We often took as much time with a relationship concern as we did with a logistical problem.

The last week before the weekend dance was stressful to many. Despite the limited responsibilities each person was assigned, many of us were worried. Our registrations were below the break-even point, but we were close enough that potential walk-ins might cause us to break even. At the last meeting before the event we meet at the church site of the event, where the issue was raised about using a smaller but more attractive room instead of the large gymnasium. We determined that with our current registrations, plus anticipated walk-ins, the smaller room would suffice. All but one person wanted to move the dance to the smaller room. That member had been a key worker and had a major role ahead. I held up the decision to talk with her about her feelings and thoughts. During a break a member of the group asked me why I was taking so long with making a particular simple decision. His girlfriend immediately spoke up and said, "Because if we go on without her feeling okay it'll be a mess." I knew it wasn't just me who knew that we needed unity. When we returned to the meeting she had decided to get on board, and we decided to use the small, attractive room for the dance.

Most of us arrived at the church quite early to set up. All was going smoothly until I picked up the Groovemongers' percussionist at the airport. His main drum did not arrive with him, and his secondary drum had been broken by the baggage handlers. We went to a drum shop and rented a drum and glued the broken one back together. It turned out that that was the only serious problem we had the *entire* weekend, and not one person complained to me that he or she did not get to dance enough.

Within minutes of the start of the dance, members of the group were grabbing me to say, "The band and caller are *great!*" Good music and calling have the capacity to lift up the spirit of people beyond what they thought was possible. They were doing that to us. More "Wows!" were expressed from our group than I had ever heard.

We were also proud to show off our Memphis personality. Unlike the atmosphere at large dance settings such as Knoxville or Atlanta where pride is in the excellence of the dance experience itself, a small group such as ours felt a pride in the warm and accepting teaching atmosphere we had created. Seth was as masterful as Martha had been at helping draw our inexperienced dancers in, making sure they were guided through their confusion. One of our new dancers told Susan, "This is a whole new world!" I believe she was exclaiming not only about the enhancement of the dance itself, but also about a profound change that was happening to our group: we were becoming a community.

Gatherings at various homes where dancers and the band and caller stayed were also times of celebration. At my house we were graced during a supper break with the band, the caller, and friends sharing in warm conversation and spontaneous music in our living room. Other hosts from our group reported similar special occasions.

Everything was going so smoothly we could hardly believe it. We kept checking in with one another thinking that something was going to go wrong—especially after the initial drum problem. Nothing. I didn't even hear a complaint about someone having to work too much that he or she didn't get to dance enough. To top it off, we found out late in the weekend that we had broken even—by $31! The dance was transforming us.

Dancing has four stages of development. It begins with the early learning phase: the steps, the arm and hand movements, and the cooperation with one's partner(s). At this stage most dancers are somewhat stiff and inhibited. Those who catch on quickly are normally those who have danced other styles before and those who best manage the natural embarrassment associated with early awkwardness and mistakes. The second stage is when the dancer reaches a free-flowing efficiency with the fundamentals of the dance style and is able to embellish steps and movements, finding enjoyment out of learning how to make the dance more expressive and creative. The third stage is when the dancer, feeling personally skilled and proficient, is able to engage one's partner in truly cooperative dancing. At this stage develops the ability to coordinate one's moves with one's partner(s). This is the phase in which group dancing really begins to happen. Dancers play off of one another, lifting the creativity and enjoyment of the dance to a new level. The fourth stage is when the dancer begins to express his or her own soulfulness in the dance. This is the artistic phase. Now the dancer is able to interpret the steps, moves, and coordination in sync with the music and the other dancers, expressing beauty itself. At this stage one is not just dancing, one is a dancer.

Good music or skilled partners can often lift a dancer more quickly to this artistic phase. Skilled partners are excellent teachers. They take dancers who are semiskilled and show them by their leads or gracefulness how to truly cooperate. Patient, skilled dancers teach a higher level of coordination to all they dance with. This is one of the beautiful aspects of contra dance weekends. Dancers of all skill levels dance together, lifting the semiskilled dancers to new heights.

Some dance groups are notorious for having a degree of snobbery about them—something semiskilled dancers are quick to notice. These groups are dominated by those who have a low degree of patience with mistakes and awkwardness, and their impatience embarrasses new dancers. Our group, however, being mostly composed of new dancers, prided itself in the opposite of snobbishness. The skilled dancers in our group *loved* teaching new dancers new moves. Of course, all skilled dancers love to dance with those of equal or greater skill, but part of the beauty of contra dancing is that with every tune one dances with every dancer in the long line. Dancers are always making adjustments for the skill level of their new neighbor.

Good music also lifts dancers' skill levels. Good music has the capacity to draw us into itself, and out of our usual inhibitions and thoughts. When dancing instinctively—not thinking as much as reacting—one is more apt to find grace and artistic expression where mere movement was. The Groovemongers offered us music that lifted our levels of expression to new artistic heights. They drew us in, watched us catch on, responded to our delight, and raised the ceiling. Good musicians playing for responsive audiences have the ability to play in a sort of dialogue with their audience. Both audience and musicians make one another better. And we both had it!

In addition, our community pride was further lifted because of Martha's calling. When she took the stage we were ripe with anticipation with how coordinated she would be with this great band. She rose to the occasion. The dance didn't skip a beat with the change in style from Seth to Martha. But it was the comments of some of the Groovemongers about Martha that really topped it off. Jane Knoeck said to many of us that Martha was going to go a long way. She added that they had played with many callers, and Martha was already one of the best. It was another moment in our community life when we all smiled at what we had. Martha was *our* caller; we raised her!

Pride can certainly grow out of proportion to reality and become haughty and narcissistic, but pride is a necessary part of the striving for excellence. If a carpenter didn't have pride in his or her work, excellence would be by happenstance. Dancers who feel pride in their artistic expression are striving for excellence and the sublime that a lack of pride wouldn't encourage. Pride is an attribute that must be surrounded by humbleness, which is no easy feat, but it does happen. We have all met people who are proud enough to do excellent work but are humble despite their achievements. They seem to understand that whatever excellence they attain is not just their own doing but is a gift from many sources—many of which they did not necessarily deserve. A community that is able to feel pride in its acceptance, openness, patience, and excellence must have that pride balanced by an awareness that it is the result of much good fortune and free gifts. Our community pride was, at its best, accompanied by the awareness that we were fortunate enough to have a number of excellent out-of-town dancers who were raising our skills, and we had Seth and the Groovemongers sharing their gifts with us. We were blessed, and much of it was not from our own efforts. A grace existed in what was happening that was beyond what we deserved. But we sure could accept it.

Dancing also has an element of sensuality and sexuality to it. All dance includes moving the body in seductive ways. It causes one to sweat and breathe in ways that are arousing. For this reason dance can lead to illicit and dangerous sexual liaisons. It can be easy to forget propriety and morality in the midst of a wild dance. Throughout much of the introductions and teachings about contra dance sexual mores are often mentioned: it's okay to touch and enjoy, but not okay to intrude upon one another's sense of sexual space. Teachers and communities try to keep sexual boundaries clear. It's often said in contra dance circles, "It's a great place to flirt without following it up later with the possible negative consequences." Weekend dances are filled with flirting. As I mentioned earlier, it would be very hard for a jealous person to dance contra with all the flirting. What makes it safe are the implied and often spoken boundaries. As far as I could see, our dancers were being respectful of boundaries, helping us to feel secure in our flirtations. When boundaries are clear, flirting is not playing with fire.

By Sunday afternoon's dance finale we were all worn out . . . but we wanted to dance just a little more! It was only to be an hour-and-a-half dance, so it must have been that we all figured we could dance with unusual frenzy for that short of a time. It was incredible how well we danced together, and when Seth closed out the dance with a large circle dance that had us all interacting in supportive and tactile ways, we were exhausted physically and exhilarated emotionally.

Afterward, we cleaned up, gave rides to the airport, and sat around and talked. As we reminisced I couldn't help but see that we were awed at how smoothly it all went, how no one seemed to have had too big of a job, and that we had a profound connection with one another. This was a community.

Sometimes community grows out of a single gift that begs to be shared. When those who possess that gift do share it, the gift itself is transformed into something bigger, something more glorious. What that is, is love. The gift of dance that we offered and that was embodied in our dances and highlighted in our dance weekend created a loving spirit that touched many of us. We truly became friends. We weren't moved by success. We were moved by love for one another.

Susan is right about dance—it is peace work. It helped us love. It helped us become friends. And, God knows, love and friendship are the foundation for peace.

Conclusion

Communities have four stages of development, then they die, leaving transformed individuals capable of joining or creating new communities. First, they begin with a transcendent *vision* that captivates a core group of people. Second, they risk *openness* and vulnerability, sharing ideas and emotions that make them all grow inwardly, uncovering personal wounds, seeking healing together, and learning together. Communities have compassion and are willing to be sacrificial. Third, they take on a *mission* that draws them into action. They learn to work together in service of others. Fourth, they *celebrate* or worship together. Finally, they die one of four kinds of deaths. Some, similar to sports teams, die because they were structured only for a short-term life. They die because their time is up. Others, such as the Church Health Center, die because they outgrow their bounds and must become institutions to carry on their mission work without the original community life. Others, such as the Springdale parents, die because they were created against some force that defeats them. Finally, some die because they cannot find a peaceful resolution to power struggles. These split apart. This was what threatened the Memphis Friends Meeting. But even in their deaths, individuals have been transformed and carry on in their lives more capable of being vital parts of new communities, sometimes even leaders or of new communities.

Each of the communities I have written about contain these four development stages, and all of them will eventually die, if they haven't already. Each of them is once again in the following sections.

The Appalachian 2,000 Milers

- Vision: Of a pilgrimage that will change their lives.
- Openness: Each day is filled with sharing and mutual reflection.

doi:10.1300/5653_14

- Mission: They walk together, share food, share skills, and protect one another.
- Celebration: They laugh and have enormous fun together.

Hendrix Runners

- Vision: To achieve athletic excellence.
- Openness: We were all deeply interested in learning how to run and how to live, with a coach who was an extraordinary mentor.
- Mission: We sought to work hard, run skillfully, and compete well.
- Celebration: We cheered for one another.

Mark Class

- Vision: To learn about the Gospel of Mark.
- Openness: In asking questions of our personal reactions, we learned to face ourselves more deeply.
- Mission: We required of ourselves a rigorous study discipline, and willingly participated in discussions and retreats.
- Celebration: We often prayed together as well as laughed.

In His Steps

- Vision: To follow in the steps of Jesus.
- Openness: They would wrestle as a community of seekers with the issues and decisions to be made, encouraging one another.
- Mission: To share in the sufferings inherent in such radical activities.
- Celebration: To worship together twice a week or more.

The Church Health Center

- Vision: To provide health care to the working poor.
- Openness: We sought to respond to one another's perception of needs as we encountered them.

- Mission: To work together, supporting one another especially as we encountered the more difficult patients and illnesses, as well as to seek solutions to the causes of problems.
- Celebration: To meet every week with time to share, pray, and listen to a theological reflection.

Memphis Friends Meeting

- Vision: To establish a visible worship alternative that encourages peace, equality, simplicity, and integrity.
- Openness: We were willing to labor with one another to truly and deeply hear one another's desires, hopes, and dreams.
- Mission: We wanted to create a sanctuary that would help us all be better people.
- Celebration: Weekly worship and special worship events such as marriages have long held us together.

Basketball Team

- Vision: To play together as a well-organized and efficient team of friends.
- Openness: All the boys were willing to learn from one another, including accepting criticism, correction, and praise.
- Mission: We grew into the realization that, if we played well together, we could win the championship.
- Celebration: We truly enjoyed the individual successes of each player, cheering one another on with great enthusiasm.

Kanuga

- Vision: To be a place where pastoral counselors could be authentic with one another.
- Openness: Every workshop, every activity encourages sharing and deep reflection.
- Mission: We try to be a community that sends one another back out to minister to others with a sense of being understood by other pastoral counselors.
- Celebration: Every day at Kanuga is filled with laughter, prayer, worship, and fun.

Dance Community

- Vision: To have an extraordinary dance experience.
- Openness: Dancing itself expressed who we really are, and the planning and preparation for the weekend simply followed the precedent our dances had set.
- Mission: We wanted all who joined us at the dance weekend to feel relaxed and touched by the excellence of the event, music, and dance.
- Celebration: As if dance itself was not celebration enough, we wanted to sit around for hours and talk about the excellence of the whole event.

Each community experience also had implicit within it a live wire—someone who offered a special kind of leadership that drew community members together. Ten Percent on the Appalachian Trail, Coach Cound, Professor Wink, Shiloh and Steven, Calvin and Jesse—all these individuals drew the community together. Not by themselves, but they created the initial spark. What they had was enthusiasm and embodiment of the vision and a willingness to let others' talents rise above their own. Coach Cound said it well when he was awarded the Coach of the Year award: "You guys did all the work. I just watched." We all knew that he did more than watch. His humble leadership was a great gift to us.

It is nice to think that communities never die, but communities are similar to people: they live and die. Some live long lives, but all eventually die. However, as with great people, the legacy of a community lives on, for communities give birth to new ideas, new vision, and add love to the world that will survive in the lives of individuals and in the creation of new communities. The death of community is far from the last word, for as communities give life they are also creating life that will live on. Communities die, but new life is resurrected from their ashes.

Shortly after our Quaker youth group took its very meaningful trip to Washington, DC, and sat on the steps of the Lincoln Memorial reading Martin Luther King's "I Have a Dream" speech, our group disbanded—died. Yet three years later I got a hint of the impact that community had on those young lives when two of its members spoke about how dismayed they were at the misunderstanding some of their new college friends had about race relations. Their interracial community life had given them a perspective on race relations that was different from the norm. Now, a decade later I continue to hear stories from those touched by that community of their exploration of different challenges, of their open-mindedness, and of their willingness to face challenges.

There have been many, many communities that have deeply influenced the world far beyond the scope of their communities, long after that community died. Surrounded by communities, Socrates lives on, as does Jesus, Saint Francis, Gandhi, Martin Luther King Jr., and many other great leaders who embody community ideas and ideals.

Communities may die, but the life they create has no end. It is this realization that gives me hope as I participate in communities that die, naturally or painfully. I know that the wisdom, life, and love created within that community experience will not die, but will live on in my life, in other lives, and eventually in the formation of a new community. Furthermore, the friendships formed in community last a lifetime.

Personally, I live from community to community. I love community life. This book is my testament to the meaningfulness of community life. I have written it because I love lifting up the joy of community life—remembering those I have participated in and hearing about other people's experiences. In addition, I sincerely hope that this book has opened your eyes to the many communities you have lived in, and that it will help you participate in the creation of new communities that will give us all more life, love, and peace. In communities we become true friends, and friends make us good people. Truly, communities give life!

References

Appalachian Trail Conservancy (2005). 2,000-Milers: Facts and Statistics. Available online at: http://www.appalachiantrail.org/site/c.jkLXJ8MQKtH/b.851143/k.C36D/2000Milers_Facts_and_Statistics.htm.

Bowling for Columbine (2003). DVD. Directed by Michael Moore. Culver City, CA: Columbia TriStar Home Video.

Brinton, Howard (1967). *Ethical Mysticism in the Society of Friends*. Lebanon, PA: Pendle Hill Publications.

Calvino, Italo (1956). *Italian Folktales*. New York: Pantheon Books.

Gibbon, E. (1994). *The History of the Decline and Fall of the Roman Empire*, Volume III. London, UK: Penguin.

Hugo, Victor (1862). *Les Miserables*. Translated by Norman Denny. Reprint, New York: Penguin Classics, 1982.

Jones, W.T. (1952). *A History of Western Philosophy: The Medieval Mind*. New York: Harcourt, Brace, and World.

Needleman, Jacob (2003). *The American Soul: Rediscovering the Wisdom of the Founders*. New York: Tarcher.

Palmer, Parker (1998). *The Courage to Teach*. San Francisco: Jossey-Bass.

Peck, M. Scott (1980). *The Road Less Traveled: A New Psychology of Love, Traditional Values and Spiritual Growth*. New York: Touchstone.

Peck, M. Scott (1988). *The Different Drum: Community Making and Peace*. New York: Touchstone.

Shelton, Charles (1935). *In His Steps: "What Would Jesus Do?"* New York: Grosset and Dunlop.

Soelle, Dorothee (2001). *The Silent Cry: Mysticism and Resistance*. Minneapolis, MN: Augsburg Fortress Publishers.

Tillich, Paul (1948). *The Shaking of the Foundations*. New York: Charles Scribner's Sons.

Tillich, Paul (1952). *The Courage to Be*. New Haven, CT: Yale University Press.

Vanier, Jean (1979). *Community and Growth*. New York: Paulist Press.

Watchel, Paul (1989). *The Poverty of Affluence: A Psychological Portrait of the American Way of Life*. Gabriola Island, British Columbia, Canada: New Society Publishers.

Wink, Walter (1973). *The Bible in Human Transformation: Towards a New Paradigm for Biblical Study*. Philadelphia, PA: Fortress Press.

doi:10.1300/5653_15

Index

AAPC. *See* American Association
    of Pastoral Counselors
    (AAPC)
Academic community, 31-34
Active hope, 74
Alda, Alan, 99
American Association of Pastoral
    Counselors (AAPC)
    Kanuga meetings, 99-107, 119
    call to leadership, 106-107
    discernment of gifts, 103-104
    hospitality, 101-103
    learning to think differently and be
        different, 105-106
    opportunities for shared work, 104-105
*The American Soul: Rediscovering the
    Wisdom of the Founders*
    (Needleman), 9
Appalachian 2,000-Milers community,
    15-21, 117-118
Athletic community, 23-30, 77

Benson, Lewis, 80
The Bible in Human Transformation
    (Wink), 31
Bonds, Barry, 6
Bowling for Columbine (documentary),
    10-11
Bradburn, Cary, 23, 25
Brinton, Howard, 77
Burstyn, Ellen, 99
Bush, George H. W., 9

Calvino, Italo, 11-14
Canada, 10-11
Christianity
    creation of, 72-75
    early, 67
Church Health Center, 41-48, 61, 62,
    118-119
Clearness committee, 54-56
Communion, 3
Community. *See also*
    Pseudocommunity
    academic class as, 31-34
    athletic, 23-30, 77, 93-98, 118, 119
    basketball team, 93-98, 119
    Church Health Center, 41-48, 61,
        62, 118-119
    dance, 109-116, 120
        contra, 109-110
        good music, 114-115
        Groovemongers, 110-111, 112,
            115
        pride, 115
        sensuality and sexuality, 115-116
        skilled dancers, 114
        stages of development, 113-114
        weekend, 110-113, 115-116
    death of, 120-121
    development, 2, 117-121
        Appalachian 2,000-Milers,
            117-118
        basketball team, 119
        Church Health Center, 118-119
        dance community, 120

doi:10.1300/5653_16

Community, development (continued)
    Hendrix runners, 118
    In His Steps, 118
    Kanuga, 119
    live wire, 120
    Mark class, 118
    Memphis Friends Meeting, 119
    Hendrix Cross Country and Track
        community mentors, 29-30
        don't stop running now, 28-29
        don't sweat the small stuff,
            27-28
        the weather is just right, 25-27
    In His Steps, 35-40, 118
    individualism versus, 6
    influences of, 120-121
    leadership, 4, 33
    "Mark" class, 31-34, 118
    Memphis Friends Meeting, 49-66,
        119
        children in, 52-53
        clearness committee, 54-56
        limits of community in relation
            to growth, 62-63
        mission, 59-61
        SAYMA children's program,
            64-66
        sense of meeting, 57
        Shiloh and Steven, 57-59
        stages of development, 52
        unprogrammed meeting, 49-51
        weddings, 54
    need for, 3
    professional, 99-107
        call to leadership, 106-107
        discernment of gifts, 103-104
        hospitality, 101-103
        learning to think differently and
            be different, 105-106
        opportunities for shared work,
            104-105
    revolving nature of, 67-82
        differences made by orthodoxy,
            79-82
        early Christianity, 67
        ethical mysticism of Jesus, 71-72

Community, revolving nature of
    (continued)
    inclusive versus exclusive
        communities, 69-71
    John's communion with the
        loving God, 75-77
    Judaism at time of Jesus,
        68-69
    mystical union and Paul, 72-75
    orthodoxy, 78-79
    as secondary in United States, 6-7
    vision, 4
    versus crisis, 1
Community and Growth (Vanier),
    58-61
Competition, against versus with, 5-7,
    30
Consciousness, 1
Continuing revelation, 80
Cound, Gerald, 23-30
    as community mentor, 29-30
    don't stop running now, 28-29
    don't sweat the small stuff,
        27-28
    the weather is just right, 25-27
    "The courage to be," 8
Crawford, Jim, 28, 29
Crisis, versus community, 1

Dance, 109-116, 120
    contra, 109-110
    good music, 114-115
    Groovemongers, 110-111, 112, 115
    pride, 115
    sensuality and sexuality, 115-116
    skilled dancers, 114
    stages of development, 113-114
    weekend, 110-113
Death, struggle with, 8
Desegregation, 8
The Different Drum: Community
        Making and Peace
    (Peck), 3
Dream Therapy Group, 44

Enron, 7
Ethics, synthesis, 2
Exclusive community, versus inclusive,
 69-71
Existential insecurity, 8

Faith, 74
Fox, George, 80
Francis of Assisi, Saint, 47
Friedrich, Hegel Georg Wilhelm, 1, 2,
 29, 80
Fundamentalism, 90-91

Gandhi, Mohandas K., 4, 84, 88-90
Gibbon, Edward, 10
Groovemongers, 110-111, 112, 115
Growth, 11-14

"The Happy Man's Shirt" (folktale),
 12-14
"The Healing of the Paralytic," 33
Hegel. *See* Friedrich, Hegel Georg
 Wilhelm
Hendrix Cross Country and Track, as
 athletic community, 23-30,
 77, 118
Hicks, Julia, 42
Hillman, James, 58
*The History of the Decline and Fall
 of the Roman Empire*
 (Gibbon), 10
Hope and Healing Center, 42, 44, 45,
 46
Hugo, Victor, 77

IAF, 87
In His Steps: "What Would Jesus Do?"
 (Shelton), 35-40, 69
Inclusive community, versus exclusive,
 69-71

Industrial Areas Foundation
 (IAF), 87
Insecurity
 accentuating of differences, 8-9
 existential, 8
 our way of life, 8, 9-10
 reasons for, 7
 role of news media, 10-11
 struggle with death, 8
Institutions, 46
Integration, 8

Jackson, Phil, 5-6
Jesus
 community surrounding, 47
 ethical mysticism of, 71-72
 following in steps of, 35-40
 Judaism at time of, 68-69
John (apostle), 75-77, 80
Jones, W. T., 45-46
Jordan, Michael, 5-6
Judaism, at time of Jesus, 68-69

Kanuga meetings. *See* American
 Association of Pastoral
 Counselors (AAPC)
Kelly, Martha, 111
King, Martin Luther, Jr., 47, 53, 84

Leadership, 4, 33-34
Les Miserables (Hugo), 77
Liggett, Marjean, 53
Lincoln, Abraham, 90
Live wire, 4, 23, 33-34, 120
Logos, 77

"Mark" class community, 31-34, 118
McDonald, Jonah, 15-21
Media, role in insecurity, 9-10
Megachurches, 48, 62

Memphis Friends Meeting, 49-66, 119
    children in, 52-53
    clearness committee, 54-56
    limits of community in relation to
        growth, 62-63
    mission, 59-61
    SAYMA children's program, 64-66
    sense of meeting, 57
    Shiloh and Steven, 57-59
    stages of development, 52
    unprogrammed meeting, 49-51
    weddings, 54
Memphis School of Servant
    Leadership, 61-62
Meredith, James, 8-9
Moore, Michael, 10
Morris, Scott, 41, 42, 43, 44

Narcissism, 34
Needleman, Jacob, 9
New Foundation Fellowship, 80

Orthodoxy, 78-79
"Our way of life," 8, 9-10

Palmer, Parker, 54-56
Paul (apostle), 72-73, 79-80
Peck, M. Scott, 3, 39, 60
Perspective, 28
Philo (philosopher), 77
The Poverty of Affluence: A
    Psychological Portrait of the
    American Way of Life
    (Wachtel), 11
Professional community
    call to leadership, 106-107
    discernment of gifts, 103-104
    hospitality, 101-103
    learning to think differently and be
        different, 105-106
    opportunities for shared work,
        104-105

Pseudocommunity, 60. See also
    Community
    and athletic teams, 93-98
    Springdale Memphis Magnet
        School, 83-91
    Gandhian principles, 88-90
    new principal, 86-87
    open education, 83-85
    parent group, 86-91
    traditional education, 85

Quakerism, 80

The Road Less Traveled (Peck), 3
Rojcewicz, Rebekah, 64

Sacrificial love, 71-72
Same Time, Next Year (motion picture),
    99
Saturn car company, 6
SAYMA, 64
SCI, 88
Sense of meeting, 57, 80
Shelby County Interfaith (SCI), 88
Shelton, Charles, 35-40, 69
The Silent Cry: Mysticism and
    Resistance (Soelle), 3, 75
Socrates, 47
Soelle, Dorothee, 3, 75
Southern Appalachian Yearly Meeting
    and Association of the
    Religious Society of Friends
    (SAYMA), 64
Spirit of the People, 1, 2-3
Springdale Memphis Magnet School,
    83-91
    Gandhian principles, 88-90
    new principal, 86-87
    open education, 83-85
    parent group, 86-91
    traditional education, 85
Stearnes, Jay, 103

Tate, Marcus, 93, 96
Taylor, Gerald, 87, 89, 91
Thru-hikers, 15, 17
Tillich, Paul, 8, 76
Trail angels, 18-19

Valjean, Jean (literary character), 77
Vanier, Jean, 58-61
Vaughan, Billy, 61-62

Volksgeist, 1
Volvo car company, 6

Wachtel, Paul, 11
Wal-Mart, 7
Watts, Alan, 73
Wink, Walter, 31-34
Wonder, Stevie, 110
WorldCom, 7

Order a copy of this book with this form or online at:
http://www.haworthpress.com/store/product.asp?sku=5653

THE SPIRITUALITY OF COMMUNITY LIFE
When We Come 'Round Right

_____in hardbound at $29.95 (ISBN-13: 978-0-7890-2985-0; ISBN-10: 0-7890-2985-5)

_____in softbound at $16.95 (ISBN-13: 978-0-7890-2986-7; ISBN-10: 0-7890-2986-3)

Or order online and use special offer code HEC25 in the shopping cart.

COST OF BOOKS_____

POSTAGE & HANDLING_____
(US: $4.00 for first book & $1.50
for each additional book)
(Outside US: $5.00 for first book
& $2.00 for each additional book)

SUBTOTAL_____

IN CANADA: ADD 7% GST_____

STATE TAX_____
(NJ, NY, OH, MN, CA, IL, IN, PA, & SD
residents, add appropriate local sales tax)

FINAL TOTAL_____
(If paying in Canadian funds,
convert using the current
exchange rate, UNESCO
coupons welcome)

☐ **BILL ME LATER:** (Bill-me option is good on
US/Canada/Mexico orders only; not good to
jobbers, wholesalers, or subscription agencies.)

☐ Check here if billing address is different from
shipping address and attach purchase order and
billing address information.

Signature_____

☐ **PAYMENT ENCLOSED:** $_____

☐ **PLEASE CHARGE TO MY CREDIT CARD.**

☐ Visa ☐ MasterCard ☐ AmEx ☐ Discover
☐ Diner's Club ☐ Eurocard ☐ JCB

Account # _____

Exp. Date_____

Signature_____

Prices in US dollars and subject to change without notice.

NAME_____

INSTITUTION_____

ADDRESS_____

CITY_____

STATE/ZIP_____

COUNTRY_____ COUNTY (NY residents only)_____

TEL_____ FAX_____

E-MAIL_____

May we use your e-mail address for confirmations and other types of information? ☐ Yes ☐ No
We appreciate receiving your e-mail address and fax number. Haworth would like to e-mail or fax special
discount offers to you, as a preferred customer. **We will never share, rent, or exchange your e-mail address
or fax number.** We regard such actions as an invasion of your privacy.

Order From Your Local Bookstore or Directly From
The Haworth Press, Inc.
10 Alice Street, Binghamton, New York 13904-1580 • USA
TELEPHONE: 1-800-HAWORTH (1-800-429-6784) / Outside US/Canada: (607) 722-5857
FAX: 1-800-895-0582 / Outside US/Canada: (607) 771-0012
E-mail to: orders@haworthpress.com

For orders outside US and Canada, you may wish to order through your local
sales representative, distributor, or bookseller.
For information, see http://haworthpress.com/distributors

(Discounts are available for individual orders in US and Canada only, not booksellers/distributors.)

PLEASE PHOTOCOPY THIS FORM FOR YOUR PERSONAL USE.
http://www.HaworthPress.com   BOF06